#STAYWOKE: GO BROKE

Why South Africa won't survive America's culture wars (and what you can do about it)

HELEN ZILLE

Obsidian Worlds Publishing

Publisher: Obsidian Worlds Publishing (sales@owpublishers.com)

Editor: House of Flying Pigs (https://www.houseofflyingpigs.com/)

Cover design: Carla Daniélle (carladanielle.jpg@gmail.com)

For my grandchildren

Contents

Glossary

Political Parties

ANC: the African National Congress, once a banned liberation movement, that has been democratic South Africa's elected national government since 1994. It also governs 8 out of the country's 9 provinces. Its leader is President Cyril Ramaphosa.

DA: the Democratic Alliance, South Africa's official opposition in Parliament, is a liberal democratic party, that governs the Western Cape province and 30 municipalities across South Africa, including Cape Town. The DA's leader is John Steenhuisen.

EFF: the Economic Freedom Fighters are a populist racial nationalist and socialist opposition party to the left of the ANC. Their leader is Julius Malema.

Other

BEE: Black Economic Empowerment, an official government policy, has been used as a cover for corruption in South Africa.

BBBEE: Broad-based Black Economic Empowerment was supposed to widen the pool of beneficiaries of this policy (but has manifestly failed to do so).

Guptas: an exceedingly wealthy Indian family with three brothers —Atul, Tony, and Ajay — at its epicentre, who personified "state capture". Through developing a close association with former President Jacob Zuma, they were able to manipulate political appointments and the awarding of state tenders to benefit their business interests. In return for these political favours, the Guptas lavished "captured" politicians with huge financial rewards in an intricate network of corruption that has contributed profoundly to state failure in South Africa.

State Capture: describes the process whereby the ruling ANC deployed its loyal "cadres" into all notionally independent state institutions, to subvert their constitutional role of ensuring public accountability, turning them instead into instruments of ANC control and patronage, and protecting high-ranking politicians from the consequences of corruption. Once the Zuma faction of the ANC had captured all independent state institutions, the Guptas merely captured the Zuma family, through which they manipulated key sectors of the South African state.

Zuptas: an elision of the words Zuma and Guptas to make a new portmanteau word, describing the combined interests of the two families in maintaining political power and access to resources, corruptly acquired.

Zuptabots: the network of linked computers running fake social media accounts, to advance and protect the interests of the Zuma and Gupta families.

Botnets: networks of computers running fake social media accounts.

Sockpuppets: fake social media personalities, operated by real people (not computers) using fictitious names, to promote political objectives.

Twirritants: a portmanteau word combining Twitter and irritants. Another word for trolls.

The Rand: South Africa's currency. At the time of writing, the conversion rate to the dollar is R14,65.

Springbok: a small buck (antelope) renowned for its exuberant leaps. It is South Africa's national emblem, and the name of our national rugby team.

SAHRC: the South African Human Rights Commission, an institution set up under Chapter 9 of the South African Constitution to promote respect for human rights, and to monitor and assess the observance of human rights, investigate and report on the observance of human rights, and take steps to secure appropriate redress when human rights are violated.

Introduction: A Note on the "Culture Wars"

Anyone exposed to advertising between 1954 and 1999 will have heard of the Marlboro Man — the rugged, cattle-rustling cowboy, living free on the frontier, an embodiment of self-reliance, grit and adventure.

The personification of masculine heterosexuality, he was probably more devoted to his horses and herds than to any woman.

Marlboro Man was created in 1954 to revive a flagging cigarette brand, and in the process, revolutionised the advertising industry. He became the icon of an era.

The famous advertisements, filmed on the open prairie and around the camp fire, sold a lifestyle rather than a product.

Its appeal made Marlboro the world's top selling cigarette, as life in the land of freedom and opportunity beckoned.

"Come up to Marlboro Country" drawled the famous payoff line.

It embodied the American phenotype, and its way of life.

Inevitably, over the years, Marlboro Man accumulated as many detractors as devotees, as resentment accumulated against America's archetypal identity and actuating values.

As the counter-mobilisation developed, spearheaded by feminists, black people, the LGBTQI+ community and their allies, Middle-America's Marlboro Men faced the first serious challenge to their undisputed position on the pinnacle of the cultural pyramid.

They were not going to surrender without a fight.

Somewhere, during the course of the escalating battle, Marlboro Man morphed into Donald Trump.

Brash, angry, and confrontational, Trump led the resistance against the onslaught on what it had once meant to be "All-American".

The Culture Wars had been very visibly and audibly engaged. Two polar opposite personifications of "the land of the free and the home of the brave" were locked in combat for America's soul.

Social media offered the ideal platform for waging this war, whence it rapidly spread across the English-speaking world.

Trump, who had started his public career as an in-your-face businessman, soon became a caricature of the populist Right.

And before long, British satire had produced the perfect counterfoil.

Her name is Titania Gethsemane McGrath, 24, as publicly performative on Twitter as Donald Trump at the height of his presidency, and as unshakeable in her convictions.

They represent polar opposites in the clash of cultures that now rages across the English-speaking world, eviscerating the moderate, liberal middle ground (which is my personal comfort zone).

Titania, on the Woke extreme, identifies as a radical non-binary, intersectional poet committed to feminism, social justice and "armed peaceful protest", according to her Wikipedia profile. She has a Master's degree in Gender Studies. Her Twitter account, with over 500,000 followers, is devoted to public posturing about the causes she espouses. Through her creator, British humourist Andrew Doyle, Titania has positioned herself as a world authority on Wokeness.

Not long ago, if you wanted to understand the two combative extremes of the Culture Wars, all you had to do was compare the Twitter feeds of @realDonaldTrump and @TitaniaMcGrath.

That simple route is no longer available because a search for @realDonaldTrump will tell you: "This account has been suspended", as Trump faces a post-presidency impeachment for allegedly using his Twitter feed to incite insurrection whilst in office.

The whole world knows how the Culture Wars are playing out in America, but its impact on other countries is less well understood.

In South Africa, it has been virtually ignored. This is a particular risk in our context, where popular "culture" merely regurgitates whatever the latest fads in America and Britain happen to be, ignoring our profoundly different context.

This book seeks to explain why, given our demography, the woke Left constitutes a far bigger threat to our constitutional democracy than the populist Right does.

And the key thesis of this book is that it would be a fatal mistake for the rational liberal Centre of South African politics to abandon the battle against Wokeness.

Liberals, worldwide including in South Africa, love to display their boldness in confronting the populist Right, but somehow slide-away when the need arises to confront the illiberal, authoritarian Left.

If we allow the "culture wars" to be waged between these two extremes, the moderate Centre will be eviscerated, with disastrous consequences for our country.

It is time for us to understand what is going on, flex our muscles, and fight back.

Splashed by the Woke Spittoon

THE LONG ARC of the universe must have been bending towards justice on Thursday 28 April 2016 for a young waitress working a double shift at the vibey Obz Café in Observatory, Cape Town's bohemian student suburb, where she earned R15 ($1) an hour, plus tips.

She had recently moved out of her flat because her two waitressing jobs did not even pay half her rent, let alone enable her to support her mother, undergoing chemotherapy for advanced cancer.

Ashleigh Schultz[1] had probably never heard of a "radical non-binary trans black activist" before.

And she certainly did not recognise him/her/them[2] when two students walked through the door of the Victorian-broekie-laced, neon-lit façade. The restaurant's décor is a visual metaphor of the contradictions of post-modernism, the religious cult of Humanities students who populate the eateries on Lower Main Road.

While Ashleigh attended the two customers with her usual politeness and attention to detail, it never occurred to her that the tips she would receive from this single meal-time encounter would enable her to pay her mother's medical bills of R30,000, donate to a hospice, make a second donation to the Animal Anti-Cruelty League (that had helped her injured dog), fix her broken cellphone, and use the remainder to further her own studies.

But it was not the generosity of the student diners who transformed Ashleigh's life. It was their nastiness.

What Ntokozo Qwabe and Wandile Dlamini said to their waitress, in writing, during and after that short encounter, led to a veritable deluge of tipping from people across South Africa and the world.

The issue exploded into public attention when Qwabe boasted on Facebook after his meal:

"LOL, wow unable to stop smiling because something so black, wonderful & LIT just happened!"

The rest of the post, written in decolonised English, explains that instead of giving Ashleigh a tip when she presented the bill at the end of the meal, they handed back the till slip with the words (in bold):

"WE WILL GIVE TIP WHEN YOU RETURN THE LAND."

"She sees the note & starts shaking," explains Qwabe's Facebook post.

"She leaves us & bursts into typical white tears (like why are you crying when all we've done is make a kind request? lol!)

The post, which has subsequently been deleted, went on to explain that a "white man" (the restaurant manager) also started to "catch feelings" when he remonstrated with them for belittling the waitress.

This puzzled Qwabe, who continued: *"The part where we take up arms hasn't even come and y'all are already out here drowning us in your white tears? Really white people. Wow.*

Moral of the story: the time has come when no white person will be absolved. We are tired of 'not all white people' and all other bullshit. We are here and we want our stolen land back."

Of course, it is entirely irrelevant to Qwabe and Dlamini that Ashleigh and her mother have never owned property and have always lived in rented accommodation.

This sort of logic does not permeate the paradigm that Qwabe and Dlamini inhabit. They regarded Ashleigh Schultz not as an individual (who happened to be facing particularly challenging personal circumstances), but as an envoy of the white "race".

Because of her pale skin, she represented all whites and whatever evil every white may have perpetrated over centuries. They judged her by the colour of her skin, not the content of her character, and certainly not as an individual human being with her own unique set of circumstances.

What's more, they (and millions of others around the world these days) describe this kind of thinking as "progressive".

Their logic was rather difficult to follow for many less educated South Africans. To most of us, like myself, this was racism, plain and simple.

While most of us just rolled our eyes, shook our heads, and got on with our lives, some rare individuals actually did something about it.

Taking the lead was Sihle Ngobese, who actually drove to the Obz Café, found Ashleigh Schultz and gave her the R50 tip that the people she had actually served refused to pay until she returned land she had never stolen.

"No matter who you are, no matter your skin colour, recognising another human being as a person with feelings is what makes us human. It separates us from animals. When we see racism, let's call it out whoever it comes from," said Sihle.

Most people saw things Sihle's way.

Roman Cabanac, who lives in Johannesburg, and Ernst Shea Kruger, a South African living abroad, followed up Sihle's gesture by starting an online GoFundMe campaign to add to Sihle's tip. Before long, they had collected R145,000 in tips for Ashleigh Schultz.

The law of unintended consequences is something Qwabe and Dlamini clearly didn't learn at university.

I was interested to find out a bit more about people like Qwabe and Dlamini, so I did a quick internet search.

Qwabe is what privilege looks like in the new South Africa. He was educated at Brettonwood School, a former model C school of excellence (presumably with many white teachers) that has, since Qwabe's time, sadly declined due primarily to fee defaulters and regular cable thefts that disrupt electricity supplies.

After matric, Qwabe went on to achieve a law degree summa cum laude at the University of KwaZulu-Natal, followed by a Mandela Rhodes Scholarship to further his studies at Oxford.

Good for him, I say, without any sarcasm at all. He could not have achieved that without seriously hard work and a lot of innate talent. His achievements are something for everyone to celebrate.

But then comes the tricky bit. While at Oxford he became a leader of the "Rhodes Must Fall" movement seeking to remove Rhodes' statue from the institution, despite the fact that he was a prime beneficiary of Rhodes' legacy trust.

Most people immediately got the irony of Qwabe accepting a highly lucrative scholarship from the Trust of an arch imperialist while accusing a poverty-stricken waitress, looking after her dying mother, of the sins of his own benefactor. Summa cum laude in hypocrisy too.

But the clincher came when, at the height of the controversy, Qwabe strenuously denied that he was the one who had demanded that Ashleigh Schultz "return the land".

The demand (which Qwabe termed a "polite request") was written, he stressed, by the radical non-binary transgender black activist, Wandile Dlamini.

So all is forgiven then. All is explained and justified.

Indeed it is, in the world of ideological pseudo-reality inhabited by Qwabe and Dlamini (together with a growing number of privileged Humanities graduates from South African universities).

This world is difficult for ordinary mortals to fathom. I have spent a great deal of time reading about it in an attempt to understand it.

I think I have grasped the basics and will try and explain them as simply as I can.

Wandile's cause, as a self-proclaimed radical, non-binary transgender activist, is to oppose the notion that the world is segregated into male and female categories. Being transgender means that you have a deep and innate feeling that you were born in the wrong body and should have been born as a member of the opposite sex. Being non-binary involves gender-fluidity, locating oneself at various points on a sliding-scale between the sexes.

I am not quite sure how transgender and non-binary categories combine, but that is probably because I am a novice in this field.

Nevertheless, I and most open-minded liberal people, have an innate empathy with transgender people, and would want them to be free to live a life they value, true to whom they feel they are.

Furthermore, most of us can relate to the fact that there is a continuum between the most "feminine" of females and the most "macho" of males. Many of us, including myself, fall somewhere in between, some more to one end of the spectrum than others.

Where I radically part company with Qwabe, however, is in his assumption that being a radical non-binary transgender activist automatically imparts on Dlamini the right to belittle another person who presumably identifies as a woman, and is ostensibly white.

How does one justify this? The answer lies in what Humanities students are being taught at Universities under the label of "Critical Theory", popularly known as "Wokeness".

Stripped of all its pretentious academic jargon, Critical Theory fuses the academic traditions of Marxism and Post-Modernism.

Critical Theory (like all versions of Marxist theory) divides the world into two main categories: Victims and Villains. The incessant struggle between good and evil, thus defined, is the motor of history.

However, according to Critical Theory, this divide is no longer along class lines, (as classical Marxists claim).

It is a struggle based on innate attributes of personal identity, with the fault-lines being race, sex, sexuality, gender identity, and disability (and as many other categories of disadvantaged minorities as one can devise).

Where these fault lines cross, is the point where people are most victimised. Hence the term "intersectionality" which features so strongly in the Post-Modern lexicon at universities, and on the social media streets of Wokeville.

The Villains, according to this doctrine, are white heterosexual able-bodied men. The Victims are everyone else, in escalating degrees of victimhood.

Another crucial point to understand is that Wokeness valorises victimhood. Victims are inherently good — and the more "victimhoods" a person can claim, the nobler they are. The white, heterosexual able-bodied man is the epitome of historical evil, perpetuated in the present.

A woke understanding of history is merely a litany of atrocities committed by white heterosexual males, pivoting on colonialism and slavery.

It is for this reason that, today, "Whiteness" still represents Prime-Evil. The sins of the fathers are visited upon the children in perpetuity, according to this pseudo-religion.

If whites want to escape damnation, and prove they are decent human beings, they must be unquestioningly woke, permanently apologetic for their very existence, and never utter an opinion that challenges any other person with more victimhood points.

For South African whites seeking to be woke, it means accepting the myth that South Africa's problems began in 1652, when the first white people established a settlement on the southern tip of Africa. According to American Wokeness, the date is 1619, when the first slaves landed.

So it should be obvious why Qwabe had to defer to Dlamini ("the radical non-binary transgender activist") as the hero of "Tipgate".

Dlamini had the highest victimhood score of everyone involved in that encounter, and therefore the most virtue points.

Dlamini's score combined black virtue points, transgender points and non-binary points, with possible extra points for potentially identifying as female on that day — which in Wokeness, is like getting a seven-letter 50-point bonus in Scrabble.

Ashleigh Schultz only had female points, but she cancelled those out when she told a journalist in the aftermath of the incident that she supported the Democratic Alliance (DA), although she added that she didn't really know much about politics.

In relation to the DA, South Africa's main opposition party, Woke logic argues as follows: because most white South Africans support the DA, it must (by definition) be evil. The fact that most of the DA's voters are not white does nothing to ameliorate this. Even when the DA had a black leader, and 8 out of 9 black provincial leaders, and a majority of black members and voters, the DA was still a white party, irredeemably infused with "whiteness".

Every black person that associates with "whiteness" automatically becomes a puppet, by Woke definition. And any white who admits to supporting the DA loses all the bonus points they may have accumulated from being female, poor, trans, non-binary, lesbian, gay, bisexual, queer, disabled, homeless, abused, identifying-as-black, or any combination of the above.

Being a member of the DA, according to the Lore of Woke, is like pulling the Monopoly card that reads: "Go to jail. Go directly to jail. Do not pass 'Go'. Do not collect $200".

So, in summary: Blackness is racist if it associates with whiteness. Whiteness is racist by definition, and can only be redeemed by associating uncompromisingly and unquestioningly with black-ness that rejects whiteness or any compromise with whiteness.

If you are still puzzled, here's an example of a person who has successfully internalised these contradictions. It is the woke Jack Markovitz, the white trust fund kid who donned a red beret, proclaimed Nelson Mandela a "sell-out", mocked the working class whites of Brackenfell in Cape Town, and urged the EFF to occupy the high-end suburb of Camps Bay.

This earned him at least some of the virtue points nature denied him through his melanin deficiency, blond hair and Y chromo-some (not to mention the trust fund bequeathed to him by his late grandfather, who served together with me as a Minister in a DA

Western Cape government). Poor Jack clearly has a lot to atone for.

It is through these contortions and contradictions that we get to the core of Woke ideology: Non-racialism is Racist.

To be acceptable in the World of Woke, you have to be *Anti*-Racist. But this is not as easy to define as you might think.

There is a major debate among the aficionados of this creed as to what Anti-Racism actually means.

Perhaps the most famous protagonists of various interpretations of Anti-Racism are two American celebrity intellectuals and writers, Ta-Nehisi Coates and Ibram X. Kendi.

Although I think they both inhabit what mathematician James Lindsay describes as a "pseudo reality" awash with anti-white tropes, they sometimes make what I consider to be insightful points.

Ta-Nehisi Coates, for example, in his early writings for *Atlantic Magazine*, for which he initially became famous, made (what I consider) a valid argument when he said that absent fathers must shoulder significant responsibility for the negative social outcomes of their abandoned offspring.

He lamented the fact that some "niggers" (his word) actually brag "about running out on their kids" — initiating a cause-and-effect chain that contributes to a street culture which includes theft, harassment, and violence.[3]

Coates also bewailed the pervasive materialism among black youth, willing to risk death "for sneakers stitched by serfs" with "price tags that looked like mortgage bills".

The cost of designer clothing and "fat-ass honeys" could turn boys into killers, he lamented.

"One misstep onto suede Pumas, and the jihad begins."

Coates certainly knows how to turn a phrase.

In one of his early essays, he also spoke of "a rage that lives in all African Americans, a collective feeling of disgrace" over violent crime and absent fathers.

I totally get that. What puzzles me is how the later Coates recanted much of his earlier analysis. No doubt he had to #StayWoke by keeping up with its evolving pseudo-reality.

Kendi, on the other hand, has always rejected the argument that cultural factors play a role in shaping social outcomes. He considers this very notion racist, and believes it is actually harmful to African Americans to propagate the notion that education and hard work can transform one's circumstances. Racial disparities are purely and exclusively the result of racism, he argues.

He scoffs at what he calls efforts to "civilize" black people rather than "liberate" them.

So what would liberation look like? According to Kendi it would eradicate capitalism, because racism and capitalism are two sides of the same oppressive coin. It will also involve the seizure of political power by anti-racists who will then correct the impact of past discrimination by reverse racial discrimination, against whites.

This idea may seem revolutionary to Americans, but we are very familiar with it in South Africa. It is called the two-stage "National Democratic Revolution", which has been implemented with determination for 25 years. Kendi would do well to find out how this is working out for the majority of black youth facing a 60% unemployment rate.

While I reject most of his ideas, I certainly agree with Kendi when he says that both black and white people can be racist.

Here Kendi finds himself at odds with almost all other "Anti-Racist" theorists, who argue that black people cannot be racist because they do not have sufficient institutional power. Prejudice, the argument goes, is only one element of racism.

Racism is actually a system based on institutionalised power that is used to oppress others. And such power is something that black people in America do not have, the Woke argument goes.

Kendi disagrees.

In an interview with CNN's John Blake dated 22 September 2019, Blake asks Kendi:

"Why do you think black people can be racist as well? You've heard of the argument that people of colour can't be racist because they don't have institutional power."

And Kendi replies:

"So generally white people say, I'm not racist, and black people say, I can't be racist. There's a similar form of denial that is essential to the life of racism itself. You have black people who believe that they can't be racist because they believe that black people don't have power and that's blatantly not true. Every single person on earth has the power to resist racist policies and power. We need to recognize that there are black people who resist it, and there are some who do not because of their own anti-black racism.

And then you have black people, a limited number, who are in policy-making positions and use those policy-making decisions to institute or defend policies that harm black people. If those people were white, we would be calling them what they are — racists. If they're black, they're no different. They're racists." (My emphasis)

Now, as we all know, almost everyone in a public policy-making position, and in positions of political power in South Africa, is black.

And if the policies themselves, and their implementation, are harming black people, then the policy-makers and implementers must, by Kendi's definition, be racist.

I thoroughly agree with Kendi, even though I won't risk saying so on Twitter, which is why I am writing this book instead.

Applied to South Africa, Kendi's logic has profound implications which I will begin to explore in the next chapter.

2

Delving Deeper into Wokeness

WHEN I STARTED WRITING this book, I was interested to discover that young people have very different understandings of the word "Woke", despite the fact that they use it so liberally.

So I decided to do a quick, unrepresentative online survey, asking my Facebook friends to tell me how they understood it.

I received over 1,400 responses.

There were many positive definitions, exemplified by this one from Lorraine Weitz Brand who said "Woke" meant "to be aware of what is going on around you. To ask questions. To seek the truth. To be conscious of what you leave behind, whether it is your words or your actions. To understand life and to realise that in this world, it is not just about you".

At the other end of the spectrum were definitions, represented by that of Thabang Tad Malatji (25) who said:

"Wokeness is the leftist/Social Justice Warriors' version of the Civil Rights Movement. They claim to be fighting for racial reconciliation and equality but what they are actually fighting for is special treatment for groups that are perceived to be oppressed. They want equality of outcomes by any means necessary, even if it means using neo-Marxist ideas such as Critical Race Theory. Being Woke is the worst thing a person can be today."

Interestingly both these definitions hit the mark — but at very different points in American history.

Having spent some time delving into the origins and use of the word, I have concluded that Lorraine's definition would have been right about 160 years ago. Thabang's is nearer the mark today.

President Joe Biden is clearly trying to reclaim Lorraine's definition as the lodestar of his Presidency and party. This quest is likely to be much more difficult than he, and most moderate Democrats, imagine.

In the years ahead, America's raging culture wars are likely to tear apart the fabric of the Democratic Party itself.

Old fashioned "do-good-feel-good" liberals will go head-to-head with so-called "progressive liberals" who reject attempts to merely make the institutions of racial capitalism more comfortable for the marginalised.

They demand radical economic transformation and regard President Biden as a short-term expedient, while they promote a candidate more suited to confronting America's archetypal "Marlboro Man", and everything he represents, in the presidential campaign of 2024.

If all this sounds familiar to South Africans, that's because it is. The ideology underlying Wokeness — the politics of racial and cultural identity, mobilised to advance the economic and political interests of marginalised groups — has flourished in different ways in South Africa for centuries.

Our big challenge, after our first national democratic election of 1994, was to rise above these contests, in a quest for a common nationhood, symbolised by our first democratic president, Nelson Mandela.

This was always going to be a tenuous and vulnerable project, but for a few short years, we seemed to be making good progress.

The impact of America's emerging embrace of identity politics could not have come at a worse time for South Africa, because it was a tacit admission that the famed American "melting pot" had failed.

It has made a reversion to racial and ethnic identity seem progressive, and perhaps unintentionally lent respectability to the politics of division, demonization, and delegitimisation worldwide.

In addition, in South Africa, it provides an ideological camouflage for crooks.

Its impact will linger long after the word has gone out of fashion.

Tracing the history of the word "Woke" in America, from when it was first used as slang for "being awake", or "remaining alert", was a fascinating exercise.

Ironically, its roots appear to stretch back to the Republican Party in the United States, when, over 160 years ago, the "Wide Awake" movement of young Republicans vociferously opposed slavery, promoted awareness of injustice, and supported Abraham Lincoln's 1860 Presidential campaign.

About a century ago, its re-emergence was attributed to the Jamaican philosopher-activist Marcus Garvey, who led the first widespread black nationalist movement in the United States. He used the term to awaken people to the reality of racial oppression.

In later years, it morphed into a multi-purpose term in black American culture, to describe the capacity to see through pretence, such as noticing the telltale signs that your girlfriend might be cheating on you.

As @Kwesi_win warned on Twitter: "if she's acting 'all good', she might be cheating. Stay Woke".

After Michael Brown, a black teenager, was shot and killed by a policeman in Ferguson, Missouri in 2014, #StayWoke became the call-to-arms of the Black Lives Matter (BLM) movement, mobilising against systemic injustice.

Unlike the Civil Rights Movement of the 1950s and 60s, BLM's battle is to dismantle dominant power structures, not seek access to them.

They reject the "cap-in-hand" struggles of the past for the accommodation of black people in the institutions of white domination.

Instead, the new Woke generation is determined to take on institutional America. Their main target is the police, whom they argue, "legitimise violence" in defence of a system developed over centuries to serve the interests of white, heterosexual, able-bodied, male Americans.

The shorthand for this "evil Empire" is "Whiteness".

According to Wokeness, Whiteness has pushed all other identities to the margins of society — blacks, gays, women, people with disabilities, transsexuals, bisexuals, fat people, queer people, and any combination of these — to the point where many have suppressed their true identities, or are made to feel ashamed of them.

"Defund the Police" became the mantra of those seeking to tear down the defence of "Whiteness".

Thus it was that the word "Woke", cut loose from its original meaning, evolved into a one-word synopsis of the latest formulation of Leftist ideology — Identity Politics — rooted in Neo-Marxism and Post-Modernism.

It is the antithesis of Martin Luther King's struggle for equality-before-the law and equal opportunity in a non-racial society, epitomised by the most famous line of his most famous speech: "I have a dream that my four little children will one day live in a nation where they will not be judged by the colour of their skin, but by the content of their character".

Wokeness inverts King's renowned liberal creed: Its dogma holds that biology defines identity and determines destiny.

Its academic label is "Critical Theory" and it has several branches, including Critical Race Theory, Postcolonial Theory, Queer Theory, and a range of academic disciplines collectively described as "Identity Studies" (by their proponents) or "Grievance Studies" (by their detractors).

Critical Theory is devoted to inverting society's conventional hierarchy of privilege in order to promote marginalised identities.

Many people instinctively relate positively to that quest, which, at its best, symbolises empathy, and the desire to include everyone in mainstream society. That's a worthy goal. We all need more of it.

So why has Wokeness become such a divisive force in society? And why has it alienated, indeed actively persecuted, so many of its potential allies?

How has Wokeness, (which claims to champion inclusion), come to symbolise extreme intolerance, in its constant search for reasons to be offended by the slightest unintentional violation of its many speech codes and behavioural taboos?

How has a movement that claims to oppose bigotry, deployed as its weapon of choice, a modern form of the medieval witch-hunt, known as "cancel culture", using social media to manufacture outrage against "offending" individuals and taking social ostracisation to pre-Enlightenment extremes?

How has Wokeness appropriated for itself the term "liberal", even as it annihilates liberalism's foundational value — freedom of thought and expression?

And how do people who consider themselves woke use terms like "Nazi" and "Fascist", without any sense of irony, to describe those who disagree with them? Most youngsters who throw these words around have only ever lived in an open society, and have no idea what fascism is, nor ever met a real-life Nazi.

Indeed, the Woke movement now exemplifies the authoritarian regimentation that characterises fascism, as they tear down statues, deface paintings, and police other people's minor "speech infringements" to enforce conformity.

Yet, they equate their struggle with the great social transitions of history, such as the abolition of slavery, and the suffragette movement to enfranchise women.

Of course, most youngsters who identify as woke are entirely unaware of the background, let alone the contradictions of the cause they espouse.

They either believe the word has a positive connotation, such as being perceptive and sensitive to the feelings of others, or they use the word ritualistically, as a self-validating label.

What started as a "sign-off" line has become a "pay-off" line, the marketing trademark of the socially conscious.

It is one of the great ironies of our time that communication technology, initially heralded for its capacity to build bridges in an interconnected world, has instead become history's most powerful instrument of division.

Rather than promoting dialogue, the dominant online tribes cast those who express dissenting opinions into outer darkness. The result is the death of rational debate, and a massive setback for social progress, which since the dawn of language has evolved through divergent perspectives.

The algorithms of Twitter and Facebook are designed to keep the antagonists trapped in their thought silos. They profile every social media user, turning them into a commodity to be used for multiple profitable purposes — from product promotion to political indoctrination.

Algorithms create online mobs, reinforcing prejudice and polarising society around almost any issue a client is prepared to pay for. This eviscerates the moderate, liberal centre of politics.

What's more, millions of the participants in these virtual conflicts are not real people. They are bots, created by a range of players to influence society in particular ways. Usually, their interests are served by sharp binary divisions.

The capacity to create political chasms has a high market value, particularly in election campaigns. We saw the tip of the iceberg in various scandals, such as Cambridge Analytica, where the personal information of millions of social media users was harnessed to mobilise antagonists along the faultlines of identity, in what has become known as the "Culture Wars".

The simple monosyllable, "Woke", encompasses all these things.

Not long ago, few South Africans had ever heard of the word. But, in a few short years, communication technology carried the Woke Tsunami across the English-speaking world.

Even a superficial understanding shows how ill-suited its assumptions are to African realities, past, present, and future.

The basic approach of Wokeness is to categorise people using George Orwell's famous four-legs-good-two-legs-bad method from *Animal Farm*. This doesn't work anywhere, but particularly not in Africa.

This becomes obvious when one looks a little more closely at what American Wokeness regards as the original sin of Whiteness: slavery.

The first trade in human beings in America occurred in 1619, when George Yeardley, Governor of Virginia, bought about 20 African slaves from an English ship docked on the Virginian peninsula.

In Africa, however, slavery pre-dated the arrival of colonialism by many centuries. As Robert Collins recorded: "The first evidence was carved in stone in 2900 BCE at the second cataract depicting a boat on the Nile packed with Nubian captives for enslavement in Egypt."

In East Africa, it is traced back to the 7th century when a burgeoning slave trade developed, with Arabs selling captured Africans to the Middle East — ten centuries before West Africans were shipped across the Atlantic to America.

By the time the colonial powers arrived in West Africa, they also found an entrenched slave trade. Indeed, it was African slave traders who provided the human cargo for the trans-Atlantic colonial merchants.

It is also an inconvenient truth that attempts to end slavery in Africa were started by a colonial power — Britain — with the abolition of slavery on 1 May 1807.

In 1833, this ban was extended to the British empire. From this date on, it was illegal for any British ship or British subject, including in its African colonies, to trade in enslaved people. It took the might of the British navy to end slavery off the African coast, although the trade in human beings continued in African countries beyond Britain's reach. Indeed, it continued in Ethiopia (one of the few countries that was never colonised) until the 1930s.

America only ended slavery 58 years after Britain — and West African slavery continued, and still exists to this day in countries such as Mauritania and Niger. It is a scandal that the first time the African Union (AU) attempted to tackle present-day slavery was in 2018. Even then, the AU failed to mention the states in which slavery continues to be practiced.

Closer to home, in South Africa, the *Mfecane* (which means "the crushing" in Zulu) initiated a period of widespread chaos and warfare among indigenous ethnic groups between 1815 and about 1840.

As King Shaka created the mighty Zulu Kingdom, his military forces unleashed widespread warfare and massive social dislocation in South Eastern Africa, resulting in domination and displacement of other ethnic groups, and the demographic and political reconfiguration of the region.

There are no precise figures of the number of casualties arising out of the *Mfecane*, but the most frequently cited estimate is between 1 to 2 million.[1]

In short, blaming "Whiteness" for all the evils of Africa makes for very poor historiography.

The purpose of stating this is not to minimise the brutal impact of colonialism across Africa, or of apartheid in South Africa — the effects of which are well documented and widely known.

It is simply to underscore the point that, in history, it is not always easy to differentiate good people and evil people on the basis of their race, let alone to continue generalising on this basis, decades, generations, and centuries later.

Apart from misreading Africa's past, Wokeness misinterprets the present, and sows the seeds of future failure, especially in South Africa.

Unlike the United States, South Africa does not have deep-rooted institutions, built over centuries, that protect individual rights, and a culture of democratic accountability.

The central thesis of this book is that the fragility of South Africa's emerging democratic institutions may be unable to survive the impact of the Woke Tsunami.

In established democracies, where the pendulum of Wokeness may eventually find its equilibrium, it might even leave a positive legacy, in the form of a more inclusive society where marginalised minorities feel free to be themselves.

But in South Africa, the culture of Wokeness has the real potential to destroy our prospects of fulfilling the vision of our Constitution as an inclusive, non-racial, prosperous, accountable democracy.

Ironically, the movement formed to protect and advance the interests of minorities in America (and across the English-speaking world), does the opposite in South Africa. It targets minorities, and provides the perfect cover for a small elite, claiming to represent a demographic majority, to deflect attention from its own corruption and governance failures.

The politics of identity provides the perfect rationale for the claim that the South African Constitution is a colonial imposition that violates and de-values indigenous systems.

And that justifies violating the Constitution – as former President Jacob and his allies in the ruling African National Congress (ANC) continue to do, on an ongoing basis.

During Zuma's presidency, their strategy involved "capturing" state institutions in order to avoid being held accountable by them. They turned South Africa into a kleptocratic kakistocracy (which is really a word meaning government by the least suitable or competent citizens), ruled by ANC cadres "deployed" throughout the state by the President's lieutenants.

As the economy collapsed and the number of citizens on welfare outnumbered those in employment, the political elite found a scapegoat in what they termed "White Monopoly Capital", and proposed "Radical Economic Transformation" implemented through centralised state control, as the solution.

This rhetoric has led to further disastrous economic consequences for the country, especially for the poor, who up until now have kept a corrupt elite in power, through their votes, to their own detriment.

Minorities who are — in the main — also passionate South Africans wanting to help make their country work for all, are starting to feel constitutionally abandoned. Many respond by withdrawing their capital and skills, and either paying privately for the services the State fails to provide, or emigrating.

We know from history what happens when demagogues turn high achieving minorities into scapegoats to disguise their own failures. It only ever ends badly.

This book is, therefore, a wake-up call to the dangers of Wokeness in the South African context, not merely for minorities, but for everyone. This book is also an attempt to support the moderate liberal and social democratic centre, comprising all races in our country, to find their voice and make themselves heard.

If we do not do so, loudly and fearlessly, we will become complicit in the failure of our democratic project. Although the odds are currently stacked against us, success is still possible.

3

The Great Betrayal

OF THE MANY famous quotes attributed to former President Nelson Mandela, none is more cited than the final paragraph of his speech on 20 April 1964, delivered from the dock of the "Palace of Justice" in Pretoria, where he stood as the "First Accused" in the Rivonia Treason Trial, facing a possible death sentence.

"I have fought against white domination, and I have fought against black domination. I have cherished the ideal of a democratic and free society in which all persons live together in harmony and with equal opportunities. It is an ideal which I hope to live for, and to achieve. But if needs be, it is an ideal for which I am prepared to die."

This paragraph was internationally celebrated, because:

1. It captures the attributes of exceptional leadership: a vision worth achieving; the enormous courage and sacrifice required to reach it; and a commitment to lead

from the front, while inspiring others to follow in the hope of a better future.

2. It condenses many of the ideas that underpin the political philosophy known as liberalism, which itself emerged through centuries of struggle, against oppression and the institutional violence of feudalism, theocracy, slavery, fascism, colonialism, and more.

In short, Mandela was promising to lead South Africa into the intellectual, institutional and cultural domain that has built, sustained and continually improved modern Western democracies.

Countries that successfully followed this route, trace their transition to modernity to the Enlightenment, a period spanning about 130 years, sometimes dubbed "the long 18th century".

This era, which extended from around 1685 to 1815, saw science and reason steadily overcome superstition. Freedom of speech and opinion gradually eroded theocratic and political dogma; believers increasingly observed their faith free from persecution; and a secular State fortified itself against enforced compliance with religious doctrines.

The importance of free markets, operating outside state control, was recognised as the basis of the "Wealth of Nations", as the title of Adam Smith's most famous 1776 treatise proclaimed. Markets, Smith argued, would be the "hidden hand" capable of improving life for everyone.

Gradually, and through periods of intense conflict, epoch-changing events occurred. Kings and queens became ceremonial figureheads, stripped of absolute power. Leaders were elected through fair, multi-party contests. Losers accepted defeat at the polls, winners accepted constraints on their power, and governments became accountable to their citizens.

The rule of law was increasingly extended to all citizens, administered by independent courts drawn from the ranks of the best legal practitioners, and millions of people, using new-found freedom and opportunities, gradually moved out of poverty into the middle class.

Slavery had formally been abolished in the West by the end of the 19th century.

Around this time, the idea emerged of a meritocratic civil service, independent of the ruling party, to serve the interests of all — not merely the politically-connected.

Eventually the franchise was extended to women, initiating a new struggle for equal access to all spheres of life and culminating in a civil rights movement that extended full citizenship rights to people of colour.

The struggle for freedom then naturally evolved to the next frontier, seeking full and equal rights for other marginalised minorities, people with disabilities, and groups collectively known by the acronym LGBTQI+.

Today we define this protracted struggle in Western democracies as Progress, an iterative, incremental, and gradual process that, despite occasional and serious periods of regression — such as the rise of Marxism and Fascism in Europe during the 19th and 20th centuries — is able to solve the underlying problems that gave rise to them.

In every crisis of clashing extremes over the past century, liberalism has been able to survive, even grow stronger, as the pendulum found its centre of gravity, and the rational centre reasserted itself. That should give us confidence as we face the current conflict between the arch-antagonists — the Woke and the populist Right — seeking to annihilate one another in the "Culture Wars".

Perhaps what we are living through now is just another episodic moment of crisis in the long gestation of what we understand by the word "liberalism" — the right of individuals to live in freedom, accepting personal responsibility to use their opportunities to improve their lives, and to care for their families and communities.

But it won't triumph unless those of us who believe in these values are prepared to stand up and fight for them, even when it is very difficult to do so.

Liberals hold that the primary role of the State is to create conditions in which all people have opportunities to use their rights and freedoms to live lives they value.

Because humans are social beings, this necessarily involves defending the right to form groups to advance particular societal objectives, without undermining the rights of others.

The conditions necessary to initiate and sustain this profound transition proved notoriously difficult to replicate in other parts of the world.

As the nations that birthed the European Enlightenment spread their colonial tentacles across the globe, intentions were anything but benign. Their purpose was conquest and wealth extraction, underpinned by an insidious racism that regarded the colonised as an inferior "race". The invaders bulldozed whatever indigenous institutions stood in their path, or harnessed them to their cause.

Whatever it took, from deal-making, bribery, co-option or force of conquest, the colonists seized what they wanted in one of the most oppressive, violent, exploitative and extractive epochs in history.

And as the colonisers built new governance institutions, they deliberately excluded the indigenous population, turning the arms of state into a tool of oppression, rather than inclusive institutions of liberal democracy.

It is hardly surprising that, with few exceptions (such as India), the institutions established by colonial powers only grew deep roots in countries where the colonialists came close to decimating the local population through acts of genocide (such as America, Canada, and Australia).

In Africa, colonialism's insidious intentions were the same, but its trajectory differed.

There were instances of genocide in Africa, such as the near annihilation of the Khoi and the San in South Western Africa, the Herero and Nama in German South West Africa and the decimation of the population of the (former Belgian) Congo.

But despite the widespread inhumanity, not all colonising powers were equally brutal, and the indigenous populations remained resilient, counter-mobilising and eventually fighting back.

Liberation struggles grew in stature and strength, and colonial powers began to recognise, in varying degrees, the injustice of the brutal disruptions they had inflicted on the lives and societies of indigenous people.

As the colonial tide receded, it generally left behind institutions of state denuded of functional substance and capacity. These "shell states" did not simply disappear, however.

On the contrary. They became the bastions of modified traditional rule, and in many instances served as the institutional bases for elevating centralised control to new levels by post-colonial governments, often in single-party systems.

The pattern that unfolded was broadly the same across most of Africa. The initial euphoria of freedom – "Uhuru" -- gave way to new systems of intolerance and oppression. In different ways, but ultimately with the same end result, liberation leaders centralised power, captured the state, inverted its institutional purpose to shield themselves from accountability, crushed opposition, deployed their acolytes to all sites of power, and used high office as a licence to loot public coffers.

Many of these corrupt "shell states" eventually became full-blown criminal states. As public disillusionment and opposition grew, elections were rigged or abolished entirely.

When autocratic rulers were deposed, it was usually through assassinations or coups, rather than the ballot box. The only hope of escaping extreme poverty was proximity to political power.

The events that accompanied decolonisation in sub-Saharan Africa terrified minorities in Southern Africa. Their fears were aggravated by such events as Idi Amin's arbitrary decree, in 1972, expelling Uganda's Asian merchant class from the country with 90 days' notice.

In South Africa, the white Afrikaner minority regarded themselves not as colonisers but as the "white tribe of Africa". They had suffered severe oppression under British Colonialism, lost approximately 28,000 women and children in, or en route to, concentration camps (out of a total Afrikaner population of 273,000 in the two Boer republics), and resisted British colonial rule. They lived in a permanent state of existential crisis, seeking to protect their cultural heritage, identity, development trajectory, and self-rule, as the winds of change, blowing southwards, reached gale force.

This created the ideological justification for the system that became notorious throughout the world as apartheid — the goal of dividing South Africa into a network of separate "states" where each "tribe" could eventually govern itself.

Like all ideologies, this was unachievable in practice without intense social engineering, enforced by a web of oppressive laws, ruthlessly and often violently enforced against the majority of the population, who overcame their own historical hostilities and ethnic divisions to resist white domination. In the process, they mainly rallied behind the African National Congress as the primary vehicle of liberation.

By the 1980s, the prospects of a peaceful transition to democracy in South Africa were not only remote, but seemingly unattainable. The unfolding logic of our country's history was moving towards an escalating racial civil war.

The situation was also profoundly aggravated by the Cold War between the United States and the Soviet Union, each seeking to extend its sphere of influence across the globe, particularly in Africa.

The extent to which South Africa's liberation movements had been drawn into the sphere of Soviet and, to a lesser extent,

Chinese influence, exacerbated the fear that democracy would simply translate into racial-nationalist socialism, with the concentration of absolute power in an African "puppet" version of the Soviet or Chinese Politburo. Such a system would align more comfortably with indigenous and tribal traditions than the power-limiting and decentralised institutions of Western liberalism.

In this context, the fall of the Berlin Wall on 9 November 1989 was a momentous event, heralding the collapse of the Soviet Union. Globally, it was interpreted as a victory for liberal democracy against communism.

The end of the Soviet Union triggered the beginning of the new South Africa.

The fear of Communist domination being exercised through its local proxy, the ANC, receded. President FW de Klerk seized the moment.

Three months after the Wall's fall, Nelson Mandela walked out of prison after 27 years, the focal point of global adulation. Hours later, cutting an imposing figure on the balcony of the Cape Town City Hall, he ended his first speech as a free man with the famous words he had used in his statement from the dock, 27 years earlier:

"I have fought against white domination, and I have fought against black domination. I have cherished the ideal of a democratic and free society in which all persons live together in harmony and with equal opportunities. It is an ideal which I hope to live for, and to achieve. But if needs be, it is an ideal for which I am prepared to die."

I was standing in a huge crowd of people just below the balcony, having waited for hours in the blazing sun to experience the historic moment, and hear the words spoken by the greatest living icon in his first public speech since his incarceration.

The impact was electric. In essence, Nelson Mandela was re-committing himself to lead South Africa on a short-cut through history to a society based on liberal democratic values — a country governed by independent institutions, answerable only to a democratic constitution; where redress and equality would be advanced through a determined focus on equalising opportunities and healing the divisions of the past.

One year later, in 1991, the final apartheid law was repealed by FW de Klerk's government. It was the Population Registration Act, defining racial categories imposed on every South African under apartheid, that determined their life chances. The scrapping of this Act was the culmination of a decade during which the legal underpinnings of apartheid had been abolished, one by one. Now the road to recovery from centuries of oppression could begin.

Most South Africans were prepared to follow the non-racial path of Mandela's vision, in a multi-party system. And most also recog-nised the urgency of the task at hand.

The Constitution that emerged from the negotiations that followed was, despite its shortcomings, essentially liberal in nature and widely heralded as "the best in the world".

On becoming president, after the landmark democratic election of 1994, Mandela made racial reconciliation the hallmark of his single term in office, convincing even the most ardent sceptics that the ANC was committed to the course the President had outlined in his public speeches.

Seemingly small gestures conveyed deep significance. The promotion of Zelda la Grange, a young Afrikaner woman working as a junior typist in the Office of the President to the position of Assistant Private Secretary to the President, and then to Private Secretary of President Nelson Mandela, based on her competence (not colour), was just one of many signals that the new government was committed to an inclusive and capable state. A state staffed by professional public servants implementing policies of a democratically elected government seeking "a better life for all".

For a few glorious years it seemed non-racialism, accountability, and above all, constitutionalism, were indeed part of the ANC's DNA.

Investment and international aid poured in, individuals and businesses paid their taxes. The ANC government demonstrated fiscal discipline and respected the independence of the Reserve Bank. Within a decade, formal employment had jumped by 50% (from 7.9 million in 1994 to 11.8 million in 2004), and the national government was budgeting for a surplus.

If we had continued on this path, millions more would have been lifted out of poverty and into the middle class within a generation, especially if the ANC had not made such a spectacular mess of seeking to "transform" public education and other institutions, using the reductionist racial yardstick that would soon define all its policies and programmes.

But despite some major missteps, our courts remained independent, the media remained free, civil society was outspoken, and the small but vocal opposition, the Democratic Party (forerunner of the Democratic Alliance), remained feisty and vigilant. Above all, the economy was growing — not at the rate it could have been had the new government succeeded in dramatically improving education and skills training — but growing nonetheless.

South Africa had, it seemed, learnt lessons from the rest of the world, and from the failed democratic transitions in other countries. The world hailed us as a miracle, a demonstration of South African exceptionalism.

The year in which everything began to change (but hardly anyone noticed) was 1997, just three years after our first democratic election.

It was at the ANC's 50th Conference in Mafikeng, that the policy of cadre deployment was formally adopted to achieve ANC hegemony (control) over the state and all its institutions.

Within a year, the party had formed a national Deployment Committee under the chairmanship of the then ANC Deputy President Jacob Zuma, who held enormous power at the crown of a cascading system of deployment committees throughout the ANC's organisational hierarchy.

The Deployment Committee advised the ANC's National Executive Committee on who should fill key positions throughout the state, from government departments at every level to state-owned enterprises, development finance institutions, and society at large. By 1999, the system was fully operational, with a mission to establish ANC hegemony over every sphere of society. It was the genesis of what would later become known as State Capture.

During this period, the party also released policy papers and draft legislation declaring that "demographic representivity" would become mandatory throughout all institutions, beginning with the public service. To conform to South Africa's demography (as it was at the time), 75% of public servants had to be African, 13% white, 9% coloured, and 3% Indian.

As James Myburgh wrote in his seminal book *The Last Jacobins of Africa*: "A basic grasp of arithmetic is all that's needed to understand that this was a plan for mechanistically replacing white with black domination or 'African hegemony' as the ANC described it."

One anecdote of many involving the "transformation" of Eskom (once among the top electricity utilities in the world in terms of generation capacity and sales), illustrates the contortions this policy required in practice.

Eskom's Human Resource Manager in the early 2000s was Ms Mpho Letlape,[1] who explained in a memorable interview with the *Financial Mail*, that her job involved hiring two new staff members every day for five years. Her official job target specified that one of these two had to be a black woman, to meet "representivity quotas".

As she spoke, Eskom was advertising for 45 engineers, 24 technicians, 20 quantity surveyors and 25 buyers. Instead of filling these posts from the skilled South Africans who had applied (because they were the wrong colour or gender), Ms Letlape reportedly recruited more than 300 black Americans during 2006/2007. A group of these recruits, sourced through a Nigerian company in New York, were reportedly registered as "South Africans" in Eskom's files, as required by the quota policy. Not long afterwards, only 68 of the 300 remained in Eskom's employ.

Apart from the R60 million in travel expenses and placement fees paid to the Nigerian consultancy during that year, Ms Letlape's 2008 salary included R2,1 million (basic) and a further R2,6 million (performance bonus shares) for meeting her transformation targets (translated into current values it would be a basic salary of R4,4 million plus bonuses of R5,5 million!).

Unsurprisingly, this was also the year that rolling electricity blackouts became the norm in South Africa. This approach, replicated across countless government departments at all levels, ensured that the first casualties were the principle of non-racialism, and the commitment to a capable state that served all South Africans.

It was only a matter of time before every state institution and state-owned enterprise would fall, like skittles, to the ANC's control through the deployment process, headed by Jacob Zuma.

He used his power with extreme skill to establish a patronage network that was soon to stand him in good stead. As he ascended to the presidency, he was already effectively in control of a captured state.

For two decades, the policy of cadre deployment has been legally buttressed by a growing number of racial laws, policies, charters, regulations and other statutory requirements.

Despite the obvious need for policies to create a more inclusive economy, the ANC's model of Black Economic Empowerment (BEE) was, from the start, a fig leaf — a faux-moral camouflage for cadre enrichment which would rapidly morph into legalised corruption.

Despite being re-branded as "broad-based" black economic empowerment (BBBEE), the policy only succeeded in massively enriching a small political and commercially connected elite, while decimating South Africa's institutional underpinnings, and destroying sectors of the economy.

The mining industry is a prime example.

Thanks to government's onerous, opaque and perpetually changing BBBEE ownership prescriptions, the SA mining sector, once the backbone of our economy, missed the global resources boom between 2004 – 2011. This, despite the fact that the boom was a once-in-a-generation commodities "super cycle" driven by China's insatiable demand for all the minerals SA has in abundance.

By forfeiting this opportunity, South Africa also lost the chance to develop the upstream and downstream components of our mining economy, which now stands as a shadow of its former self.

Instead of investing in new mines and expansion to take advantage of the boom, mining companies were engaged in crazy contortions to retain their operating licenses by meeting the constantly-shifting ownership requirements of the sector's "Mining Charter", the BBBEE instrument governing this sector.

One of the more absurd but illustrative examples was Gold Fields' 2010 empowerment deal which, guided by then President Zuma's lawyer, simply gifted shares to a list of 73 hand-picked individuals, including the then Chairperson of the ANC, Baleka Mbete, and two convicted criminals, Kenny Kunene and Gayton McKenzie, to meet the Mining Charter's ownership requirement.

The only party that consistently and vociferously exposed and opposed the "re-racialisation" of South African law, since its inception in 1997, and the consequent decimation of the capable state, was the small Democratic Party (DP), and its larger successor, the Democratic Alliance (DA).

Incomprehensibly, instead of being recognised for its prescience, the DA has been largely vilified by most of the English media and much of civil society, which fell into line behind the ANC's baseless allegations that opposition to its deployment schemes and racial laws were motivated by racism, and a desire to protect white privilege.

Much of the private sector became deeply complicit and compromised in this process, and the international community, that had once so vociferously opposed apartheid, now remained largely silent.

The consequences of similarly self-serving "transformation" policies and programmes in other sectors of the economy put a freeze on private investment. Poverty had grown beyond anything that could have been imagined back in 1991, as had the structural barriers to economic inclusion.

It was a betrayal of all South Africans, but most specifically of the vast majority of black South Africans who had overwhelmingly pinned their hopes on the ANC to create conditions that would enable them to overcome poverty and unemployment.

At the height of apartheid and in the face of full-blown sanctions against South Africa, official unemployment stood at 10%. After 25 years of ANC rule, the percentage of people unemployed and actively looking for work reached 30%, and that was before the jobs decimation of the Covid pandemic.

Youth unemployment is close to 60%.

Today, South Africa's staggering unemployment rate is primarily the result of policies and laws that enabled the ANC's NEC, advised by its deployment committee since 1997, to institutionalise patronage, to entrench party control over all notionally independent institutions, to obliterate the separation between party and state, to gain access to all major capital flows in the country, to legalise corruption, and to ultimately make the transition to a full-blown criminal state inevitable.[2]

By 2009, there were already fewer South Africans in jobs than on welfare, and the disparity has grown ever since, with employment taking a substantial further knock during the Covid crisis.

South African exceptionalism has been exposed as a myth. Instead, the country is following the well-trodden path to state failure and growing impoverishment that was a feature of the majority of transitions from authoritarian rule in Latin America and Africa during the previous century.

A central thesis of James Myburgh's book, referenced earlier, is that to understand ANC rule, one must focus on the documents it adopts in its internal meetings and the speeches made to in-house audiences, not those directed to the media and the rest of the world.

Piecing these together, he shows that the driving "motive force" behind the ANC's actions and decisions was a commitment to the doctrine known as the National Democratic Revolution (NDR), adapted from Soviet revolutionary theory during the 1960s and officially adopted by the ANC at a conference in Morogoro in 1969.

The strategy was published in January 1963 in the Journal of the South African Communist Party under the title "The Road to South African Freedom: Programme of the South African Communist Party". It described the foundational concepts of the ANC ideology, most specifically the NDR.

Having read this document during his doctoral studies, Myburgh concludes that the ANC's actions in power, became "not just explicable, but predictable".

Although hundreds of thousands of words have been devoted to analysing the NDR, it can be summarised in four clear points, some explicitly stated, others revealed in practice:

- The ANC must exercise hegemonic control over all institutions of State.
- The State must extend this control over society, as well as the commanding heights of the economy.
- To achieve this end, the ANC must deploy loyal cadres to commanding positions in all centres of power.
- Political power is a legitimate means of capital accumulation.

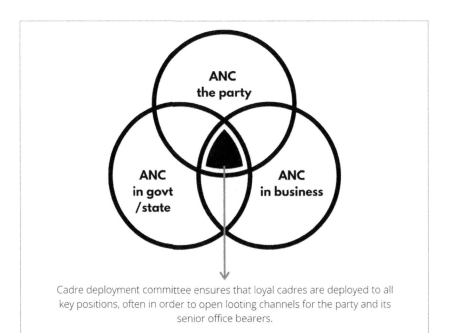

Cadre deployment committee ensures that loyal cadres are deployed to all key positions, often in order to open looting channels for the party and its senior office bearers.

The process that led from centralisation of power to cadre deployment, corruption, state capture and finally to the criminal state, was not an accident. It was the result of a conscious strategy which reached its apogee under former President Jacob Zuma. Its foundations had been set out in the ANC's internal documents, and government practice, from the very start.

Indeed, from the mid-1990s, the ANC was open about its determination to control all state institutions and their resources in the interests of the party, which it equated with the interests of the people.

As Joel Netshitenzhe, a leading ANC intellectual, wrote in the ANC mouthpiece *Umrabulo* in 1998: The aim of the National Democratic Revolution (NDR) "is extending the power of the 'National Liberation Movement' over all levers of power: the army, the police, the bureaucracy, intelligence structures, the judiciary, parastatals, and agencies such as regulatory bodies, the public broadcaster, the central bank and so on".

The ANC's deployment policy aimed to achieve party control of the state. And then, through the state, over every other sector of society by introducing stricter and stricter laws mandating black empowerment and "employment equity". This enabled deployed cadres to burrow into almost every money flow and every stream of public funding in the country.

The blurring of boundaries between party and personal funds during the ANC's years in exile did not improve on the road to the seat of government in Pretoria's Union Buildings.

On the contrary, new sources of funding became available, as private sponsors flocked around the ANC's leadership en route to powerful positions in the state.

As the ANC undertook the transition to power, its leaders became the beneficiaries of substantial largesse from individuals and corporates. Initially, this practice was excused as compensation for the sacrifices of the years in imprisonment or exile. Gradually, the distinction between generosity, gratitude, and corruption fell away.

From the first ANC administration, the practice had been established that senior politicians could live well beyond their means, supported by the patronage of their wealthy connections.

As ANC politicians increasingly assumed the right to live lives of luxury, the only way to do it was by looting the state or selling their influence. This is how corruption became endemic.

The notion of a low-key middle-class lifestyle for people in positions of power became unthinkable.

And the notion of being held to account by state institutions the ANC controlled was strongly resisted.

The world and most South Africans, especially the media, chose to believe what the ANC said to selected audiences, not what it was planning in the privacy of its inner sanctums.

Of course, the primary victims of the ANC's policies were the (predominantly black) poor, who depended on a functional, capable state for the opportunities (ranging from running water to good education and health care) they needed to improve their lives.

The middle class, and especially white South Africans, largely had the means to insulate themselves from state incapacity, reflected in an explosion of private service provision across the health, education, and private security sectors in particular.

In effect, this involved paying double taxation, first to a state failing to provide satisfactory services, and second to private sector providers.

When the DP and the DA, often largely alone, pointed out this great betrayal, it was labelled a "white party" defending "white privilege" even though, objectively speaking, the primary consequence of this betrayal of public trust was a majority of black people sinking deeper into poverty and unemployment. This, while the magic inner circle of ANC deployees became fabulously wealthy, largely as a result of the legalised corruption — known laughably as broad-based black economic empowerment (BBBEE) — rather than the result of enterprise or innovation.

Jacob Zuma, who had initiated and overseen the process of cadre deployment between 1997 and mid-2005, ascended to power as president on a tidal wave of support in 2009. This only became possible after serious corruption charges against him had been incomprehensibly and unlawfully withdrawn — a stark illustration of the consequences of cadre deployment in a key institution of state – the National Prosecuting Authority.

But instead of heeding the alarm bells, the media predictably pilloried the DA as racist for its election slogan in 2009, calling on voters to "Stop Zuma".

Within three years of his ascendency to the presidency, the ANC NEC's Policy Committee issued a statement on 5 March 2012 saying, in paraphrased summary, that the "bourgeois revolution" (involving the seizure of the primary levers of power) was sufficiently complete to enable a transition to the second stage of the NDR on the road to socialism.

This two-stage theory of revolution, adopted by the ANC at its Morogoro Conference of 1969, postulated the notion that underdeveloped countries must first pass through a capitalist stage, via a bourgeois revolution, before moving on to full-blown socialism.

The ANC continued to act as though its internal policy documents trumped the Constitution. It was a betrayal of their public commitments, to the people of South Africa, and to the world.

One would have thought that this would have elicited increasing local and international resistance, especially as the DP, and later its successor, the DA, had pointed out what was going on from the start.

Since the late 1990s (after reading two seminal books — *Transitions from Authoritarian Rule* and *The Criminalisation of the State in Africa*)

— I regularly spoke of the succession of "Cs" that would inevitably follow each other as the ANC institutionalised cadre deployment behind the smokescreen of BEE and later BBBEE:

1. The Centralisation of power in the Party;
2. Cronyism (Cadre deployment);
3. Corruption and
4. The Capture and Criminalisation of the State.

It was only years later that the media began to use the concept of "State Capture" (although they still largely misunderstood it). While there were exposés aplenty of corruption, there was in general, a stubborn refusal to go to the root of the problem and call it by its name: Broad-Based Black Economic Empowerment.

To expose and oppose this was still, despite all the evidence, pilloried as racism and the protection of "white privilege". As a result, most analysis of State Capture was deliberately superficial and focused on Zuma, so as to avoid exposing the fact that successive ANC administrations had deliberately and meticulously captured and hollowed out the State over a period of nearly three decades.

To this day, most institutions that were united and outspoken in the anti-apartheid struggle, including the English media, the liberal universities, the majority of civil society organisations, and the international community, have been ominously silent on this cause-and-effect trajectory of South Africa's decline.

The captured, criminal State was not the result of "pilot error" in an otherwise noble endeavour. It was the inevitable outcome of the re-racialisation of South African politics and law.

A few brave individuals and organisations have spoken openly and strongly to expose what is going on. Tragically, many others have been complicit in South Africa's slide towards a Failed State.

Even the media, which has exposed so much of the corruption that was the inevitable consequence of cadre deployment (disguised as BBBEE), rarely challenged the foundations of this policy. They only focussed on the consequences.

But even then, one would have thought that the policies that gave rise to this situation would be assiduously re-examined, and the principle of non-racialism re-asserted.

Instead, the very opposite has happened, and very suddenly too.

I would pinpoint the date to around 2015, when the very concept of non-racialism, so essential for halting cadre deployment and South Africa's slide into a failed state, became itself the target of attack and was described as "racist".

The commitment to non-racialism came to be regarded as a barrier to inclusion — and a reason to escalate race-based preferencing to the point of imposing quotas. The only consequence was escalating unemployment and impoverishment.

This seemed completely incomprehensible to me at the time. Non-racialism was the lodestar that had guided the struggle against colonialism and apartheid. It is one of the founding principles of our Constitution.

But suddenly, inexplicably, to support non-racialism meant admitting to being "racist".

This was rationalised by the argument that, despite political liberation, the vast majority of black people remained excluded from the economy.

But, as I have shown, BBBEE was never intended as a mechanism for economic inclusion. It was, from the outset, a fig leaf behind which connected cadres and their fellow travellers could get very rich indeed, while their corruption destroyed prospects for sustainable growth and job creation — merely creating more exclusion and poverty.

When the DA re-committed itself to non-racialism at its policy conference of September 2020, most of the commentariat in the English media expressed their shock and horror.

As Andisiwe Makinana noted in her "wrap" of the political year in the *Sunday Times* of 27th December 2020, the DA had "stunned" South Africa by adopting a resolution embracing non-racialism. That summed up much of the mainstream response to our landmark conference.

Once again, the DA stands largely isolated, with a few notable exceptions among NGOs, in openly reaffirming and defending its commitment to non-racialism.

I could have foreseen many scenarios for South Africa. But what I could never have predicted was that, within a single generation of the ANC coming to power, it would have become the custodians of the politics of racial identity — the very philosophy that had underpinned apartheid.

Even less would I have predicted that the vision Nelson Mandela had repeatedly stated at pivotal moments in the struggle for democracy, would not only have been abandoned, but actually labelled as "selling-out".

And this is where I return to Ibram X. Kendi's logic, referred to in the previous chapter:

"... You have black people," he said "who are in policy-making positions and use those policy-making decisions to institute or defend policies that harm black people. If those people were white, we would be calling them what they are — racists. If they're black, they're no different. They're racists."

He's right. The ANC has turned out to be among the biggest racists ever to rule South Africa.

Using unemployment and the Gini coefficient as the yardstick of whether or not life is getting better for the majority of black South Africans, the ANC would perhaps rank even worse than the apartheid government (not even I would dare to tweet this, but it is actually true). The ANC has passed more race-based laws that locked more poor people into permanent poverty than apartheid did. That is a simple and tragic fact.

One would think that this would prompt a major re-examination of the policies that have led to this dire situation, and an analysis of the major blockages to investment and job creation, in an effort to improve things.

But one would be wrong.

As has happened in many countries throughout history, it is easier to search for a scapegoat (and there are a few easily to hand), such as whites, Indians, and entrepreneurial foreign nationals.

There are historical precedents aplenty for the tendencies of failing populist governments to blame minorities instead of facing up to their own responsibilities, the most famous historical examples being the Jews in Germany, and the Tutsis in Rwanda.

One would also think that a new generation of young South Africans, emerging from some first-rate universities, would have learnt from the past, and sought to avoid repeating these historic mistakes.

Again, one would be wrong.

Why has South Africa's new generation failed to learn from history, and has their finger firmly on the "rewind and repeat" button instead?

The next chapter ventures a tentative explanation.

4

Caging Minds

AS A DEVELOPING DEMOCRACY where access to education and skills remains confined to a relatively small proportion of the population, South Africa feels the impact of what is taught at its higher education institutions far more immediately than established democracies.

And this applies particularly to what is taught in Humanities faculties.

These disciplines rarely attract the top students, but disproportionately produce graduates destined to exert profound influence over societal culture.

After three years of immersion in the potent Woke marinade-mix of Marxism and Post-Modernism, these students move into the "high-human-contact" professions: Media, teaching, human resources, non-governmental organisations, the performing and visual arts, advertising, corporate social responsibility, politics and many more.

Those who remain at university to specialise in professional degrees, such as law, often build on this foundation too.

And because of South Africa's drive to achieve rapid racial transformation, many young black Humanities graduates rise very swiftly through the ranks of the organisations they join, influencing not merely the direction and the culture of the enterprises that hire them, but the culture of society as well.

A similar phenomenon has been unfolding in the United States, but more gradually and imperceptibly, over a much longer period. This process underlies the "Culture Wars" that are now tearing America apart.

As the voice of Wokeness grew louder and more extreme, labelling anyone who disagreed with any part of their dogma or methods as "racist", "fascist", and "Nazi", the moderate liberal middle ground was either bludgeoned into silence, or sought refuge to the right, looking for protection from a leader bold and brash enough to tackle Wokeness head-on.

It was this reaction against Wokeness that, I believe, played a key role in bringing Donald Trump to power in the 2016 US presidential election. Trump rode the frustrations of middle America, who felt crushed by every recession, and left behind by every economic boom.

People who dared not express moderate opinions lest they be deemed offensive to the Woke thought-police wanted someone who would not be intimidated into silence. There was no candidate more brazen than Trump.

Wokeness contributed directly to decimating the moderate liberal centre, fuelling its polar opposite, the populist Right, and bringing it to power in America.

Four years later, the election of Joe Biden is an indication that the pendulum of American politics may be finding its centre once more, which is good news for the rest of the world that has been swept up in America's Culture Wars.

But it is far too early to reach this conclusion. One of President Biden's greatest challenges will be to resolve the profound cleavage between liberalism (properly defined) and Wokeness inside his own party.

Will he be strong enough to reassert Enlightenment values and an inclusive rational liberalism as the core belief system in the Democratic Party?

Seeking to do this will be a formidable challenge, because it is not in the nature of Wokeness to debate issues logically or rationally, nor to respect the rights of others to proffer a different opinion.

In fact, in many ways, Biden's victory may well embolden the Woke wing within the Democratic Party.

Whatever the outcome, it will have a profound effect on the trajectory of Wokeness in the rest of the world, including South Africa, through the interconnectedness of higher education institutions, but more particularly, through the power of social media.

"Sharing the internet with America is like sharing your living room with a rhinoceros. It's huge, it's right there, and whatever it's doing now, you sure as hell know about it," wrote Helen Lewis in *The Atlantic* (October 27, 2020).

So how did the Woke Rhinoceros arrive so suddenly in South Africa's collective living room, somewhere around 2015?

Our first direct public encounter with it was at the University of Cape Town (UCT) where "FeesMustFall" mutated into "Rhodes-MustFall," which itself quickly morphed into a movement to "decolonise" universities, including libraries and works of art.

Woke ideology had already been simmering for a while in the cauldron of various specialised areas of "identity studies", which examine the "lived experience" of marginalised identities (gender, trans, queer, disabled, fat etc.) to give them a voice against the dominance of the "Cis-het patriarchy" (their preferred term for white, heterosexual males).

These dissenting voices joined forces in the collective effort to "decolonise" what was South Africa's premier university.

It would be wrong to claim the Woke mob ignited a "culture war" at UCT. Rather, they forced a swift surrender during the preliminary skirmishes, following a short siege by a militant few. As has been the case in many other universities globally, neither UCT's Vice-Chancellor, nor the University Council, nor the silent majority of students, could find the courage to stand firm against Woke militancy.

Ironically, just as Wokeness driven by a minority of students drowned out all other voices at UCT, the liberal Democratic Alliance Students' Organisation (DASO) had just won a student representative council election on campus with an outright majority.

The young DA liberals could fairly lay claim to being the legitimate voice of elected student leadership. They were in the perfect position to draw a line in the sand.

But without a clear steer from the party's leadership, and taken aback by the speed, intimidation, and violence of the decolonisation movement's debut, DASO floundered, fell silent, or was otherwise cajoled and cowed into line behind Wokeness.

To make matters worse, the newly elected DA leader, Mmusi Maimane, strode onto campus seeking "street cred" with the protestors, before being unceremoniously bundled off, leaving the elected DA student leadership even more confused as to how they should respond.

It must be said that the University of the Witwatersrand's Vice-Chancellor, Professor Adam Habib, was one outstanding exception to the general rule of surrender among universities. He was able to draw a distinction between the genuine crisis of affordability for poor students, and those who merely saddled the fees protest to make the campus ungovernable in order to "disrupt existing hierarchies of knowledge and power".

He knew the militant mob was determined to bring the university to its knees, and he was determined it would remain standing.

Habib devised a way around the belligerent minority by holding a referendum on campus on the issue of whether to suspend classes, thus giving the majority a voice — which was resoundingly in favour of ending the Woke shutdown and resuming classes.

But that sort of leadership was a rare exception.

The *Zeitgeist* shift initiated by Wokeness happened so rapidly in South Africa that it suddenly became impossible to say things that, just a few months earlier, were considered to be rational propositions, as I will show in the next chapters.

It is true that every generation is challenged by their progeny. Confrontational thinking from young, bright people is necessary and positive. It is what drives social progress, especially if (as the Humanities claim) they teach students to "think outside the box, to deal with problems and find solutions as well as being critical and questioning of the world around them."[1]

But, in fact, Humanities faculties at many South African universities (following a trend across the English-speaking world) tend to do the opposite.

Far too many Humanities degree programmes serve to construct a mental cage, ironically called "Critical Theory", designed to prevent students from thinking critically about what they are taught to believe, silencing anyone who disagrees with them, and insulating their minds from the complexity of reality.

Because this ideology has been elevated to the status of a religion, reality must either be forced to fit its frame, or rejected, and ignored.

This ideological fanaticism sends young graduates into the world uniquely ill-equipped to grapple with complexity. It also makes it a taboo for universities, through their research programmes, to interrogate many of the critical challenges facing our society in any meaningful way. Merely asking difficult questions often violates the norms of Woke.

Helen Pluckrose, a liberal political and cultural writer, and editor of *Areo* Magazine, together with James Lindsay, a mathematician with a background in physics who founded the online Journal *New Discourses* (with the magnificent tagline "Pursuing the light of objective truth in subjective darkness") have teamed up to write an excellent guide to Critical Theory.[2]

Cynical Theories is a very readable yet dense and sometimes complex book, which I highly recommend to anyone interested in learning more about this topic.

For my short book, I am focussing on a few of their key points. Please bear with me for a few pages, because an understanding of the basics is essential to fathom what is currently going on in our society.

I have selected the following points from Pluckrose and Lindsay's work:

1. Wokeness is "Applied Post-Modernism".

2. Post Modernism, in turn, centres on two core principles:

   a. A Knowledge Principle and
   b. A Power Principle

3. Social Justice flows from these two principles. It is a core concept in Woke ideology, which through post-modern knowledge and political principles, seeks to radically transform society.

4. The method involves identifying specific issues and driving them in ways that are aimed at confronting and fundamentally changing the power hierarchies, structure, and functioning of society.

I will try to explain these concepts as simply as I can, hopefully without doing them an injustice, by using concrete examples.

The Knowledge Principle

Wokeness rejects the idea that there is such a thing as objective knowledge and truth.

Dominant cultures and groups, they argue, construct truth and knowledge to defend their interests. Wokes reject the scientific method as the primary method of testing the validity of a thesis, or getting closer to truth, because this process lends authority to dominant cultures.

And they reject the liberal approach to research because it revolves around getting closer to understanding reality rather than fundamentally changing it.

This is why knowledge must be "decolonised" i.e. stripped of the methods and content used in Western societies over centuries, because they are obstacles to achieving Social Justice in the world.

Despite its rejection of the idea of objective truth, Wokeness is premised on its own central and supposedly objective truth, which is that oppression based on biological and cultural identity, lies at the root of society's inequities.

While rejecting the notion of the free and autonomous individual as the primary unit of value in society (the traditional liberal view) they elevate individual "lived experience" to a higher standing in research and analysis than scientifically verifiable facts.

This differs from the liberal notion that, even though it may be hard to attain, there is such a thing as truth. Liberalism holds that no one has unique access to the truth, but that human beings can move closer to the truth, through testing and challenging ideas and observations against available evidence.

Liberals accept that it is more difficult to reach truth in the social sciences than in the natural sciences, because human beings are complex and irreducible to reliable equations that can be applied in all comparable cases.

Humans respond differently to the same stimuli, and are driven by different motives. But liberals still believe there is a core reality in each situation, and that it is possible to get closer to it through evidence and understanding (what sociologist Max Weber called *Verstehen*).

Through seeking to examine and understand actions and behaviours and their consequences, it is possible to move closer to reality — and this makes a significant difference to social outcomes, as any person in a decision-making position can tell you.

Liberals believe that the key purpose of universities is to transmit accumulated human knowledge, to test that knowledge against new discoveries, evidence and ideas, and to roll back the frontiers of knowledge through research.

This leads to incremental change in society, as human beings seek the truth, apply its lessons, and extend its benefits to growing numbers of people. It may be a gradual form of change, but it is a sustainable, reliable and non-violent way of extending social justice.

Wokes believe that this definition of the university serves to sustain existing power hierarchies. The purpose is not merely to understand and incrementally improve the world, but to radically revolutionise it.

The Power Principle

This is the Woke belief that society comprises a system of power hierarchies, which determine what can and should be known, and how events and actions should be interpreted.

These unequal power relations are inherent in every interaction and in every situation, whether this is apparent to any of the participants or not.

It is the job of Critical Social Justice activists firstly to expose these unequal power relations, and then to dismantle them.

Indicators of unequal power relations include racism, sexism, homophobia, transphobia, fatphobia, ableism, and every other prejudice that has been built into the structures and systems of society over centuries by the guardians of the "norm" — white, heterosexual males.

And even if none of the participants in an interaction is aware of any prejudice, it is there, subliminally, and must be unearthed and eradicated.

Wokeness thus seeks to identify the Villains and Victims in every situation. Social Justice in action involves exposing, shaming, and crushing the Villains, while supporting and empowering the Victims.

One of the ways unequal power relations are maintained and recognised is through what Wokeness calls "discourses" — the way that people speak about other people, ideas, topical issues and events. For far too long, Wokeness argues, white heterosexual males have framed societies' discourses in ways that preserve their own dominance.

It is for this reason that Social Justice activists are always on the frontline, policing other people's language, and on the lookout for any suspicious word or phrase that could be interpreted as perpetuating the discourse of dominance. Where they find it, they move in for the kill.

In the Lore of Woke, "Language is Violence", and must be met with counter-violence.

The first casualty of this doctrine is free speech — the very foundational value of liberal societies. According to the liberal view of the world, progress hinges on the dialectic method: argument and counter-argument.

Obviously, in this process, people will say things that other people do not want to hear, and may even find highly offensive. But because freedom and progress depend on the right to say offensive things, liberals place a very high premium on free speech.

There is not a single liberal constitution in the world which states that a person has the right not to be offended.

Of course, Wokeness says a lot of things that liberals do not want to hear, but being liberals, we listen because we understand that however offensive an idea may initially sound, it could contain a kernel of truth which could advance our understanding of society and the world. Indeed, I myself have discovered this as I did research for this book.

There is a lot of sense, for example, in the proposition that human beings socially construct what they understand as reality, and there is validity to the concept of "lived experience" (although it cannot be elevated to absolute truth).

But "listening" doesn't work the other way around. No one may say anything that falls foul of the speech codes of Wokeness.

When I read about the "Violence of Language", I understood why self-appointed Social Justice Warriors spend so much of their time trawling through other people's social media posts looking for any telltale sign of dominance, any violation of the Woke Narrative, or any other reason to feel offended.

And I began to understand why their response seemed so disproportionate to the perceived offence.

Because they construe language as violence, Wokes genuinely believe it is entirely appropriate to respond with commensurate force by "cancelling" offenders from society entirely. The bigger the fish they can bring down, the better.

For them, I was the "Big, White, Anti-Woke Whale".

As soon as they pick up the scent of offence, the woke pack hunt begins, conscripting an army of real people, their sock puppets, and bots on Twitter, Facebook, and Instagram. Not to mention their ever-willing servants in the mainstream media, and every other *noch-schlepper*, (a magnificent Yiddish phrase my parents used to describe every tag-along-pain-in-the-butt).

Once the whole network is mobilised, the price the "offender" pays is so high that everyone else has been warned: never, ever dare to offend Woke speech codes, not even unintentionally. And don't dare stand up and defend someone who is being "cancelled".

In fact, being able to "cancel" offenders, to the point of getting them fired from their jobs, and preferably cast out of mainstream society too, is a badge of honour, equivalent to a military medal for valour in the internal Woke hierarchy.

If you do it publicly enough, you could even have a starring role in an online video, which explains the performative nature of cancel culture.

—▭—

"Fuck Free Speech" shouted a student collective at Evergreen State College in the state of Washington in the US, which instantly achieved their objective of trending on Twitter and YouTube.

The video ends with a trans person saying sarcastically and to rousing applause: "I am so sorry, but your free speech is not more important than the lives of black, trans, femmes, and students of this campus".

It is worth dwelling for a while on the events that led to this trending video at Evergreen State College — a place I had never heard of before the Rhinoceros in our living room drew it to my attention.

The Woke insurrection started after a Dr Bret Weinstein, who had taught evolutionary biology on the campus for 14 years, objected to a call for every white person to absent themselves from the campus for a day, in order to create a "safe space" for black people, and to give white students and staff an understanding of what it feels like to be "excluded".

Weinstein, who self-defines as progressive, wrote an email to fellow faculty members objecting to the "segregationist agenda". The most offensive words in his email were *"One's right to speak or 'to be' must never be based on skin colour"*.

This has always been the progressive liberal creed.

But, predictably, it caused woke outrage. His students shouted him down. They demanded that he be fired. They refused to even listen to his argument for non-racialism. They called him a racist who had forfeited the right to speak at all.

"He has validated white supremacists and Nazis and that should not be protected by free speech," said a young white student calling for Weinstein to be fired.

"He can go and be a racist shit somewhere else," said another.

Weinstein was determined to continue teaching, and when "Social Justice" activists disrupted his lectures, the campus police refused to intervene to protect either his right to do so, or his students' right to attend his classes.

So he continued lecturing in a nearby off-campus public park and sued the university. Both he and his wife resigned after reaching a financial settlement with the Evergreen State College.

Videos of every stage in this horror story were sent around the world, and of course it was not long before South African students were staging similar productions for the world's social media platforms.

One that shot to prominence was aptly titled "Science Must Fall".

When I first watched it (without understanding Wokeness) I dismissed it as embarrassingly idiotic.

When I watched it again, after reading Pluckrose and Lindsay's book, I understood that it reflected the Woke paradigm perfectly.

The video shows a student-led seminar in what seems to be a lecture room at the University of Cape Town.

The contributor, a young black woman, speaks:

"If you want a practical solution on how to decolonise science, we have to restart science from an African perspective, from our perspective of how we experience science," she ventures.

Hearing some mutterings around the room she continues to describe a place in KwaZulu-Natal (I think she said Umhlabuyalingana) where people believe it is possible to send lightning bolts to strike down an enemy using magical powers.

"Can you explain it scientifically?" she asks.

At which point a male voice can be heard shouting: "But it's not true".

A male (and likely white) voice talking about scientific truth in a Woke seminar is like frying pork sausages on a gas cooker in a mosque or synagogue during Friday prayers.

His interjection was perceived as an assertion of the "scientific method" which supposedly devalued her "lived experience". This underscores why Wokeness rejects words like "true" especially when uttered by white males. After all, according to Wokery, their "truth" serves merely to uphold a hierarchy designed to keep them in power.

The chair of the meeting, who also appeared to be a woman, put this interloper firmly in his place, telling him the venue was a "safe space" — safe presumably from white, male, heterosexual discourses.

Order restored, the speaker continues: "Western modernity is the direct antagonistic factor to decolonisation. Because Western knowledge is totalising. It is saying that it was Newton, and only Newton, who saw an apple falling out of a tree and then out of nowhere decided that gravity existed and created an equation and that is it.

Whether people knew Newton or not, or whatever happened in Western Africa or Northern Africa, the only way to understand gravity is through Newton who sat under a tree and saw an apple fall.

So Western Modernity is the problem that decolonisation directly deals with, to say that 'we have knowledge that speaks to us, and that is able to accommodate knowledge from our perspective'."

When this video went viral, most viewers thought it was a spoof.

Now I understand that it makes total sense from within the paradigm of Critical Theory. The lived experience of people who believe that magical powers can throw lightning bolts to wipe out their enemies is, from the Woke perspective, as valid a form of knowledge as Newtonian physics.

All I can say is that, if this young woman lives in KwaZulu-Natal, and if she ever flies home via King Shaka airport, she will be able to depend on the reliability of Newton's laws of motion for the aeroplane to get off the ground and to land safely.

If she were ever to hope that lightning strikes a rival-in-love, and seeks the help of the experts in Umhlabuyalingana, the outcome will be less certain.

And if universities take these arguments seriously (except for studying their cultural, psychological, and behavioural impacts on communities), they will be irreversibly on the road from Woke to Broke.

In this, they will be following in the footsteps of the English print media.

A few years back, the once-mighty *Independent* newspaper group deliberately made racial transformation combined with a Woke interpretation of society, the lodestar of its editorial approach. Primarily as a consequence of this, they have lost readers by the thousands, and their circulation has dropped so low as a result, that they have become effectively irrelevant to public debates on topical issues. Many other titles are following suit.

This cannot be attributed merely to the rise of social media. The same level of readership decimation has not happened to newspapers that have upheld the traditional approach to their role, reflecting facts as accurately as possible and separating news from commentary, to serve their readers.

My intention in writing this book, however, is not to deride Wokeness. It is to understand it better because it is, in my view, the biggest threat we face to achieving the promise of our Constitution, based as it is on Enlightenment values.

Of course, Wokes are right to say there are power hierarchies in every society. Indeed, power hierarchies enable human societies to function rather than succumb to the forces of entropy and chaos.

And, of course, power hierarchies are open to abuse in every society.

Power hierarchies that perpetuate injustice, exclusion, and inefficiency, and that inhibit new ideas and innovation, are certainly not confined to Whiteness. They should be challenged wherever they manifest themselves. This is crucial for social progress.

Liberalism seeks to hold power to account through institutions that prevent abuse, and enable the citizens, through free speech, persuasion, and ultimately the ballot, to replace those hierarchies through peaceful rather than violent means.

Free speech, an independent judiciary, strong and functional public institutions, and a vibrant self-regulating media are essential institutions in preventing power abuse.

In contrast, Wokeness seeks a hierarchy-free society, in which the collective is king. But as we know, all historical attempts to create classless, hierarchy-free societies have led to more persecution, violence, oppression, and death than any system that instead tries to regulate and moderate power hierarchies through fair and transparent rules.

Wokeness is in fact a secular religion, and as such it needs rules and a creed. Who determines these? Who enforces its dogma?

If the answer is "the most vulnerable in society through their own lived experience", then the question arises: who are the most vulnerable? And how do they enforce their codes?

Ironically, there is already a growing internecine conflict within the internal hierarchies of different vulnerable identity groups that populate the engine room of Wokedom, as to who gets to decide what is permissible, based on the accumulation of the most victimhood points. So don't hold your breath for the imminent arrival of the hierarchy-free society under Wokeness.

The Woke Revolution is already experiencing hunger pangs for its own children.

But while they may not be able to agree on what they stand for beyond generalities, like most social movements, Wokes of all stripes can agree on what they are against, and who the Villains are that must face collective retribution.

And it is to their methods of attack that I now turn.

5

The Politics of Personal Destruction

THE "TRADITIONAL WEAPON" of Wokeness is personal destruction.

The purpose is to make "an example" of a high-profile person who is deemed to have violated woke speech (or behaviour) codes so that no one else dares to do so again, for fear of the consequences. That is part of how the Woke enforce rapid, revolutionary social change in the world.

The politics of personal destruction always involves high drama, which is an excellent distraction from the real issues a society should be facing up to. That is why this method is so popular amongst those who preside over failing states or institutions. The best counter strategy is diversion.

The "politics of personal destruction" can be devastatingly effective, and always works in stages, as I set out below.

By definition, it targets individuals rather than groups or institutions, because individuals are particularly vulnerable, especially if they can be isolated from their support group, and preferably from society too.

It is a vicious and cruel form of social and political action, but in most cases, it works.

Having studied several cases, I have identified the steps that the politics of personal destruction follow. They do not always happen in the same sequence, but when the ball starts rolling, things move very quickly, often overnight, and this contributes to overwhelming the chosen target.

The first step is to identify a violation of the woke narrative (or behaviour code).

Step two is to decontexualise what was actually said or done, and distort (even edit or misrepresent) it to convey the most offensive possible meaning.

Step three is to amplify the wilful distortion by mobilising a range of networks, especially social media, to manufacture as much "outrage" as possible.

This third step requires some elaboration.

As social media's penetration of society grew, it didn't take long for IT entrepreneurs and political strategists to spot a market gap to assist governments, political parties and lobby groups in using social media networks to destroy their opponents and distract attention from their own failures.

Here was a huge opportunity to sell a service that would monitor one's opponents' narratives, or even create fake narratives, define them as offensive, and then amplify them to create as much division, diversion, polarisation, and alienation as possible.

"Divide-and-Conquer" has always been part of the armoury of war and politics, but never before had it been able to harness so powerful a technological tool.

This created a whole new industry known as troll farming. Every day, hundreds of people around the world would show up to work in an adapted form of a call centre, where their job was to amplify social media messaging through botnets (networks of hundreds of linked computers) in order to inflict maximum damage on a client's adversaries.

The strategic brains behind these operations were companies like Cambridge Analytica and Bell Pottinger, who offered clients the service of formulating the most divisive and polarising messages possible, to weaken their opponents.

Unsurprisingly, one of their key offerings was reputation destruction and public shaming.

Step four is to ensure the manufactured outrage is picked up by the mainstream media. This is easy enough to do, as the media, in recent years, have followed social media looking for news items like a dog follows a bitch in heat. There is nothing like a trending case of "personal destruction" to bring out the media vultures. Once mainstream media join the fray, the outrage somehow becomes "official". The issue grows wings and can fly for weeks.

Step five draws in the woke columnists, media commentators, and academics (the *noch-schleppers*) to opine about the gravity of the situation, lending credence to the idea that the offender deserves to be cast out of polite society. This helps divert public attention away from the actual pressing issues in society.

Step six involves laying complaints against the "offender" with every official structure around. In South Africa, the options are many and varied: You can lay a charge with the police for "hate speech", complain to the Human Rights Commission, the Equality Court, the Public Protector, or the Independent Communications Authority. Even if you know the complaint has no substance, the very fact that there is such a complaint blows new life into the controversy and keeps it trending.

Step seven is to seek to isolate the offender from support networks by getting their colleagues/family to publicly dissociate from them, and preferably join the witch hunt. In politics, one's fiercest opponents are often inside one's own party — and unsurprisingly, can usually be found amongst the key instigators of outrage manufacturing.

Step eight involves demanding an apology, which is then used as proof that a serious violation has occurred, which justifies the extent of the outcry, making the persecution seem appropriate. If you apologise, then—

Step nine involves rejecting the apology as insincere, not far-reaching enough, or whatever, paving the way for —

Step ten, during which demands for resignation/firing escalate.

By this time, organisations and companies have usually lost their nerve, and the strategy succeeds. The target loses their job.

As the organisation tries to "mop up" the reputational damage, *Step eleven* comes into play.

This involves various forms of "sensitivity training" and the formulation of "Codes of Conduct" or "Brand Guidelines" that add a new transgression to the existing list of offences.

Step eleven makes it an offence to give offence.

Even liberal organisations have difficulty understanding how dangerous this is, and what a victory they are handing to the illiberal social justice warriors when they capitulate.

There is a very good reason why no liberal Bill of Rights anywhere in the world gives anyone the right not to be offended, as I have explained already.

By shaming just one individual publicly, the Wokes succeed in enforcing their speech codes on an entire organisation, and incrementally, on an entire society. It thus becomes taboo even to raise crucial matters that should be debated in order to address the underlying causes of intractable societal problems, lest the discussion falls foul of "The Narrative".

Who, for example, would care to suggest that we research why it is so difficult to end the practice of having multiple concurrent intergenerational sexual partners (despite widespread knowledge about how HIV is transmitted)?

This is one of the key reasons that we only deal with HIV through treatment, rather than prevention. And this is costing the state billions annually that we cannot afford.

Behavioural change would require a level of social capital (understanding and acting on the likely consequences of one's actions on others) which unfortunately is seriously lacking in our society, despite the much vaunted notion of "Ubuntu".

Merely saying this will bring a raging torrent of abuse down on one. Is it any wonder then that our universities are not researching many of these crucial, if sensitive issues?

But this is a digression.

The issue I am trying to deal with here is this: How should an individual who is being targeted for personal destruction respond to this vicious and predictable cycle described above?

Having accumulated quite a bit of experience over the years on this subject, my advice is:

1. Recognise what is happening. Being the target of an orchestrated "cancelling" initially flattens you like a tidal wave from behind. At first, you will literally not know what hit you, and you won't be able to find ground beneath your feet.
2. Remain calm. You will resurface. Try not to internalise what is being said about you.
3. Ask yourself whether you have really said or done something unacceptable, using the yardstick of truthfulness and your personal ethical code, or whether you merely disrupted a woke narrative.
4. Accept that the people who love you, or work with you, will panic. Remain undeterred. There is no reason to "catastrophise" issues. It only makes things worse.
5. Do not resign. If your organisation won't defend you, wait to be fired and fight your case.
6. If you can afford it, get a lawyer to stand by you, especially if your job is threatened. If you cannot access a lawyer, seek the advice and support of someone whose rationality

and judgement you trust, especially if you are feeling isolated. The Constitution and the law support your right to freedom of speech even if the mob doesn't.

7. Do not try to reason with online botnets. They couldn't care. They are paid to do the job of destroying you. You can explain until you are blue in the face that what you actually said is not what they say you said. You can expose the motives behind the decontexualisation and distortion. You can even expose the bots themselves. It will make absolutely no difference.

8. However, be prepared to stand firm and fight back. Do make a reasoned statement setting out the facts, and set down your contextualised argument in rational articles in the mainstream media (while expecting irrational responses). At least your case will be there for those to read who do not wilfully wish to misrepresent and misunderstand you.

9. If you believe that what you said is true, do not apologise. Apologies tend to make things worse because an apology justifies the attack in the first place. And people who are absolutely determined to be offended (usually on behalf of other people they don't even know) won't accept apologies anyway. Their purpose is not reconciliation. It is enforced submission and annihilation.

10. If an apology is the price you have to pay to keep your job, make up your own mind. I have no right to advise you on this. However, it is always worth remembering that your apology may well be the first step on the road to losing your job, and can be used against you as an acknowledgement that you committed a major error.

I myself have apologised for saying things that are true, but it was not to keep my job. It was to protect someone else's, which I shall explain in the next chapter.

Many who read my advice above will validly ask: How does this help? How could this see me through the torture of being publicly cancelled and vilified? How would I be able to face the world again?

These are valid questions. I was therefore delighted to learn that the indomitable Helen Pluckrose, working with others, has formed an organisation called Counterweight to help individuals resist the impact of "Critical Social Justice" (Wokeness) in their daily lives.

Counterweight comprises a network of support teams and action groups including parents, teachers, psychologists, social workers, technicians, academics, and other professionals all devising practical ways to support each other and protect people against this authoritarian tide.

After reading through the content on their excellent website (https://counterweightsupport.com/why-was-counterweight-formed/), I joined the movement immediately and am determined to support and promote their work in South Africa where it is needed more than ever.

Indeed, we need to start their South African branch.

In this chapter, however, I have a more limited objective — to explain what happened to the economist Chris Hart, one of the early South African targets of Cancel Culture.

His background is interesting. In the early 2000s, he became known for his Afro-optimism, as he was generally really upbeat about South Africa's future.

We were well on the way to getting the fundamentals right, he argued. The Rand kept strengthening, and we were on our way to creating sound conditions for investment, growth and jobs. He gave me, among many others, hope for the future. He became one of a small group of economists who were "public influencers" as well as market strategists.

He played a prominent public role through his independent commentary, before being headhunted by Standard Bank as a Global Market Strategist in September 2015.

When Jacob Zuma ascended to power, Chris saw South Africa's prospects for job-creating growth evaporate, and like many of us, was intensely worried about helping South Africa turn the corner. Social media, the hangout of the young, seemed a crucial tool for Chris to utilise, in order to convey core ideas that challenged Zumanomics.

Chris's influence soon became apparent when he rapidly accumulated 21,000 Twitter followers.

December 2015 marked the nadir of Zuma's "reign" when he fired Nhlanhla Nene as Finance Minister, replacing him with Gupta acolyte, Des van Rooyen.

The Rand crashed and markets went into a tailspin, wiping out an estimated R500 billion in value overnight. It was one of those rare occasions where big business actually mobilised collectively to persuade Zuma to retract his controversial appointment, and replace van Rooyen with the more experienced and respected Pravin Gordhan as Finance Minister.

Late that Sunday night, a journalist phoned Chris Hart for comment. He offered his critical analysis. Political non-alignment had always been a point of principle with him, in order to maintain analytic credibility.

This criticism was not well-received by the ANC, and set the scene for the start of 2016, in the run-up to the local government elections. The ANC needed to drive the politics of diversion in order to mobilise voters around race, not service delivery.

Chris started the year with a series of 40 tweets to outline the economic challenges of South Africa. After setting out the problem, he reflected on the implications for our greatest crisis — unemployment — and how to confront it.

In those days, Twitter only allowed 140 characters per post, which was fine for crisp direct interaction, but not for nuanced analysis, particularly not in a single tweet. That is why people often posted several tweets on a single topic, to cover their bases. What Chris couldn't say in one tweet, he could say in 40.

But, as I explained above, a key tactic of the politics of personal destruction is "decontextualisation".

Conveniently for the Wokes, Twitter enables one to pick out a single tweet from a series (even a few words from a single tweet), and elevate it to the only thing that was said, twisting it to give the most egregious interpretation possible.

One of Chris' tweets said: "More than 25 years after Apartheid ended, the victims are increasing along with a sense of entitlement and hatred towards minorities."

This may be a controversial point of view, but it is a perfectly legitimate one, particularly as part of a series that also said things like:

"Apartheid is SA's national scar. But unemployment has become a bigger scar. SA needs saving, investment, and growth."

"Unemployment needs employers. If 10-15 million new jobs are needed, then 3-4 million new businesses are needed. Businesses employ. Infrastructure doesn't."

And so on.

But unwittingly, in just three words of a single tweet, Chris had handed the ANC the diversion they were looking for. These words were "sense of entitlement".

The mob moved in to denounce Chris as a "racist" (what else?).

Twitter erupted, and the hysteria started spurting forth, like ash and lava from a volcano.

As it turned out in a series of stunning revelations much later on, it was exactly around this time in January 2016 that Duduzane Zuma was meeting personally with Victoria Geoghegan, a senior Partner in Bell Pottinger. This British PR company was to set up a "reputational management" contract to boost the flailing fortunes of his father, Jacob, and the Gupta-faction of the ANC.

The contract, to the value of R2 million per *month*, was to be paid through funding channelled via the Guptas, Duduzane's employers.

According to leaked documents, the key message in the run-up to the crucial 2016 elections (and beyond) would be that "economic apartheid" and "White Monopoly Capital" were the reason that the majority of South Africans were poor and getting poorer. And that only the ANC under Zuma could salvage the situation through Radical Economic Transformation.

The purpose of this narrative was to counter the growing perception that unemployment was caused primarily by the ANC's policy incoherence, a failing state, corruption, lack of investment, capital flight, and uncertainty regarding property rights.

In a letter to Duduzane after their meeting, Geoghegan wrote that "it is critical that the narrative grabs the attention of the grass roots population who must identify with it, connect with it, and feel united by it.

The key to any political messaging is repetition and we will need to use every media channel that we can to let our message take seed and grow and [make people] feel united by it.

The narrative should appeal to both potential third-party activists in the business and academic communities and the grass-root population." Geoghegan certainly understood the value of the *noch-schleppers* in the commentariat.

She also promised that Bell Pottinger would work "shoulder to shoulder [with Zuma] in communicating such a vital message for South Africa".

The Chris Hart debacle happened during this period, a short while before the contract with Bell Pottinger was finally signed.

And although I cannot prove it, I suspect Bell Pottinger may have had a hand in the incredible speed with which the call went out to "Black Twitter" to "roast" Chris Hart, for his tweet, one in a series, that revealed why government policy and state incompetence (not "White Monopoly Capital") were responsible for the rapid escalation in unemployment.

In other words, Chris was conveying the direct opposite of the communication mandate given to Bell Pottinger on behalf of the Zuptas.

But whether Bell Pottinger was involved or not, it would be a very interesting exercise to see how many of the Twitter accounts used in the mob assault on Chris were bots, and how many were real people. I am prepared to bet the bots outnumbered the warm bodies.

In any event, the outcry on social media was totally disproportional to the offence, and created the diversion the ANC wanted. The hysterical reaction achieved its objective by creating the impression that the real problem in SA was white racism, white monopoly capital and "economic apartheid", not an incompetent government seeking a looting channel into the very heart of the Finance Ministry through the appointment of a Gupta acolyte to head it.

Chris, seeing the tsunami of negative responses, issued an apology at the end of the tweet series: He had never intended to cause offence, he said, "for which I apologize wholeheartedly". His apology, he emphasised, was for having given offence, not for any of the tweets themselves.

That was the equivalent of Twittercide. In one fell swoop, it justified the outcry. He had himself admitted that he had "caused offence"! The chorus of voices rose commensurately.

The next morning, the ANC ratcheted up the Hart "crisis" several notches by laying criminal charges against him.

Pouring fuel on the fire, Standard Bank released a statement which claimed that Hart's comments were "factually incorrect, make inappropriate assumptions about South Africa and have racist undertones".

When Chris went to work the following day, he said it felt like "walking into a deep freeze". The social ostracisation had worked instantly.

The next step was a letter to Standard Bank staff, which was also published in the media, from Sim Tshabalala, the bank's CEO. It read:

"Racist opinions are usually weapons in the struggle for resources. Some white people, for instance, appear — despite the provisions of our Constitution and our laws — to be tempted to argue that poor black people are not entitled to various goods because they are 'dirty' or because they have a 'victim mentality'. Some black people seem to think — despite the values and principles stated in our Constitution — that white people are not entitled to be full citizens because they are 'all racists'. As can be seen from these examples "entitled" is often a key word in racist thinking".

I have scoured Chris's series of tweets repeatedly and nowhere do I find any suggestion that he was even implying that "poor black people are not entitled to various goods because they are 'dirty' or because they have a 'victim mentality'."

Quite the contrary. From the context it is clear that the entitlement he is referring to is the rent-seeking behaviour of people who want to reap rich rewards from the combination of their political connections and the colour of their skin, at the expense of the poor.

But, losing his nerve, Sim Tshabalala continued the decontexualisation and demonization. The script was playing out perfectly.

James Myburgh, the editor of *Politicsweb*, wrote an excellent analysis on this debacle titled "A descent into racial madness" (14 January 2016).

"In the early weeks of January, much of the South African intelligentsia descended into a state of what can only be described as racial madness. There was a loss of all sense of reality, proportion, consistency, fairness and common decency," he wrote.

"Although some of the fever has now passed, this episode once again displayed a disturbing inability by many of our institutions to remain cool, stand firm, and do the right thing under social media mob pressure."

He then asked the absolutely valid question. Why, overnight, had the words "sense of entitlement" become taboo?

The answer is that it disrupted a woke narrative. If all the ills and dispossessions of the world can be explained by the existence of white males, then a sense of entitlement for everyone else, especially those who can lay claim to multiple victimhoods, is entirely valid. For a white male to suggest otherwise is a clear example of "violent language".

For Wokes, the very fact that Hart, and then Myburgh, were speaking as white males on a sensitive subject, was an act of violence in itself.

Undeterred, Myburgh listed numerous examples where the words "culture of entitlement" had been used in a negative context by a range of influential individuals, including former Presidents Nelson Mandela and Thabo Mbeki, cabinet ministers and even that high priest of South African Wokery, journalist Eusebius McKaiser.

In other words, the concept of "a culture of entitlement" had been the subject of legitimate public debate for decades. Yet suddenly, overnight, it was weaponised to create a diversion for the ANC to destroy a prominent critic of Zuptanomics.

The warning to others could not have been clearer. The chilling effect on open discussion about important topics was immense.

Unsurprisingly, big business fell silent. It tends to do that, unless of course, R500 billion is wiped off the stock exchange overnight.

Standard Bank pressed for Chris' immediate resignation. He refused, and negotiated an exit package.

This moment symbolised far more than his exit from Standard Bank.

It symbolised a dark period in South Africa's political history, between 2014 and 2017, when public debate was shaped by shadowy forces who were being paid large amounts of money to manage messages over interconnected computers to drive the politics of person destruction.

During this period, the ironically named *Independent* newspaper group, as well as countless social media accounts, seemed to be permanently on the lookout for anything that could be presented as proof of "white racism", in order to generate as much outrage as possible. Chris Hart's experience was not the first, nor would it be the last.

It was during this period that hashtags such as #CapeTownIsRacist were driven relentlessly, in order to delegitimise the democratically elected government of the city.

This confected outrage was anything but "organic". It was carefully orchestrated behind the scenes, aided and abetted by a surfeit of useful idiots. The Bell Pottinger revelations merely exposed what had already been underway for some time.

The penny finally dropped for me when, in January 2021, Dr Sydney Mufamadi, a former cabinet minister who had led a high level investigation into the country's State Security Agency, gave evidence before Judge Raymond Zondo (who is, at the time of writing in February 2021, heading a Commission of Inquiry into corruption and "state capture" in South Africa).

Dr Mufamadi dropped one bombshell after another, as he announced how millions had found their way through the State Security Agency's slush funds into projects to protect and promote the political fortunes of former President Jacob Zuma.

These included projects to buy off judges to deliver judgments in favour of Zuma, as well as journalists to promote the former president's cause. Dr Mufamadi specifically mentioned an amount of R20 million being siphoned into the Africa News Agency, owned by Iqbal Survé, who is also the proprietor of *Independent* newspapers. Survé has also benefitted to the tune of billions from state institutions, specifically the Public Investment Corporation that enabled him to buy the *Independent* Group for R2 billion and turn it into a propaganda stable for the President's war against "White Monopoly Capital" and in favour of "Radical Economic Transformation".

This is undoubtedly the tip of the iceberg of the money involved, and of the extent of the paid "influencer" network that drove this propaganda campaign.

Little did I know back then (although I should have suspected), that I was high on their hit list.

The extent to which I was in their crosshairs came home to me when a former member of President Zuma's high level security team asked to see me in late September 2020.

We met at a quiet suburban coffee shop. He told me he had turned to God, and I presume this is what had led him to tell me what had been going on behind the scenes.

"The ANC spent a lot of time trying to find something they could pin on you," he said. He then told me how he and others had been involved in scrutinising companies that secured tenders while I was Executive Mayor of Cape Town to see whether any of my family was being enriched.

"No matter how hard we dug, we could not come up with anything," he said.

"The ANC was particularly worried about you because you had appeal across population groups, and you had led the DA (Democratic Alliance) in taking Cape Town from the ANC and later the

Western Cape. They were anxious that after that, you would become leader of the Opposition in Parliament and continue from there."

"When they could find nothing to pin on you, they made you the target of a smear campaign through social media. We knew you were outspoken on Twitter, and so we just waited. Everything you posted was analysed. After several attempts, it worked. The DA eventually took the bait, and turned on you. Then the ANC knew they had won."

The next chapter tells that story.

6

My Own Story

DURING MY TEN years as Premier of the Western Cape, I was privileged to be able to take several trips abroad, together with government and business representatives.

Our primary purpose was to establish partnerships and promote trade and investment. But the most valuable aspect of these trips was the lessons we learnt from other countries.

In early March 2017, following 18 months of mayhem at South African tertiary institutions based on demands for "decolonisation", I just happened to be heading for a visit to Japan and Singapore.

One of the key lessons I've learnt each time I've gone abroad, is the extent that culture shapes a society — but this subject is taboo in South Africa.

Simply raising the issue violates every Woke narrative there is.

Landing in Asian countries requires significant cultural adjustment, like an astronaut getting used to the absence of gravity.

Take Japan for instance.

One of Tokyo's problems, I learnt, was that there wasn't enough crime to keep the police busy.

Instead of lazing around watching series, or eating KFC, Japanese police were intent on finding any possible form of crime to prosecute, in order to feel deserving of their monthly salaries.

The most minor infringements are treated with forensic thoroughness, including the prosecution of a graffiti artist who had painted a Hitler moustache on a poster of the prime minister.

Another case involved the mysterious disappearance of a pair of panties from a washing line. Its owner alleged it had been stolen.

People were starting to complain that the police had become overzealous, and were infringing on their freedom.

It is an extraordinary feeling to be in a country, even for a few days, that has effectively conquered crime.

I learnt how, following the devastation of World War II (that destroyed about 40% of Japan's industrial plant and infrastructure), many Japanese actually came to regard the American occupying force as a blessing.

It was during the American occupation that Japan undertook essential social and economic reforms in order to become a modern industrial economy, and in particular, enabled rural areas to escape feudal land tenure systems.

This laid the basis for one of the most effective developmental states in history — although their definition was fundamentally different to the South African version.

They described a "developmental state" as a highly efficient, meritocratic state that creates conditions for investor confidence, aligning every policy (and its efficient implementation) to maximising conditions for economic growth.

This was the state that enabled Japan to rise so rapidly from the ashes of war.

But it was Singapore that most fascinated me.

Everywhere I went, there was something named after Sir Thomas Stamford Bingley Raffles: from hospitals and research institutes to technical colleges and the swankiest hotel (we didn't stay there).

In Singaporean history, Raffles is roughly the equivalent of Jan van Riebeeck and Cecil John Rhodes combined. He was the Lieutenant-Governor of the Dutch East Indies on behalf of the British Empire. It was Raffles who landed on the banks of the Singapore River in 1819 as the lead coloniser.

I learnt with complete astonishment that several years *after* independence from Britain, Singapore had unveiled a statue to honour Raffles, on that very landing spot. It has since become one of the most iconic tourism sites in the city-state.

Having just lived through the frenzy of #RhodesMustFall back home, I asked people I met why Raffles shouldn't suffer the same fate.

Without exception, they looked at me in complete astonishment. After some discussion, I found some people prepared to concede that Raffles' statues should perhaps be complemented by others, to honour a wider cast of contributors to Singapore's development. But #RafflesMustFall? Never!

Time and again I was told that Singapore honoured Raffles because of the foundations he had laid for the emergence of modern Singapore. Without his insight into the exceptional strategic value of its location, and the capacity of its port to become the pivot of an international trade, logistics, and transport hub, Singapore would not have evolved into the powerhouse it is today.

After hearing versions of this answer several times, I stopped being surprised. I had grown accustomed to weightlessness.

I learnt that, at independence in 1965, Singapore was far less well-endowed with natural resources than many African countries. Its major problem back then, like ours is today, was unemployment.

Within 15 years of independence (less than a single generation), Singapore "had left [its] old problems of unemployment and lack of investments behind," wrote Lee Kuan Yew, Singapore's post-independence leader, in his memoirs.

The Lee administration's relentless future focus, its refusal to compromise on meritocracy or tolerate corruption, and its determination to build on the institutional foundations the colonists had created, turned it into a magnet for investors and entrepreneurs worldwide.

The result was a growth rate that brought unemployment down to 1.8 percent by 1997, 32 years after independence.

There was, I concluded, a lot we could learn from countries like Japan and Singapore, rather than merely mimicking the latest fads from America and Britain.

When I returned from these trips, I would always contribute to a report for our government, as well as articles for more popular consumption.

Being active on social media, with close to a million Twitter followers at that stage, I also shared my distilled insights with them, knowing that the majority of social media users would not get around to reading a serious article on geopolitical lessons for South Africa.

The fact that about half of my followers were fake accounts (according to the free online apps that estimate these things) was something I did not realise at that stage. I genuinely thought I had almost a million *real* human followers!

I was also completely unaware of the contract that the Zuptas had signed with Bell Pottinger, and its implications for anyone with a high enough profile who stood in their way.

And I certainly could never have predicted that the last in my series of four tweets would start a chain reaction that would make the Chris Hart affair look like a Teddy Bears' Picnic.

Over the course of a week in Japan and Singapore, I had become so accustomed to having rational conversations that I required an astronaut's phased decompression to return to South Africa's dense atmosphere.

During just one week away, I had forgotten that we only pay lip service to equal citizenship and free speech in our country. In reality, every opinion is judged on the basis of the skin colour of the person who expresses it.

In Singapore and Japan, I was an individual making a point. In South Africa, "speaking while white" on a controversial race-laden topic is considered the ultimate sin.

At the time, I hadn't heard of the term "Wokeness" yet. But, looking back, I now know exactly what my transgression was:

I had disrupted a Woke Narrative through the Violence of my Language.

My series of tweets, posted on the morning of 16 March 2017 (when Twitter still only allowed 140 characters per post) read:

"Much to learn from Singapore, colonised for as long as SA, and under brutal occupation in WW2. Can we apply the lessons in our democracy?"

"Singapore had no natural resources and 50 years ago was poorer than most African countries. Now they soar. What are the lessons?"

"I think Singapore lessons are: 1) Meritocracy; 2) multiculturalism; 3) work ethic; 4) open to globalism; 4) English; 5) future orientation."

"Other reasons for Singapore's success: Parents take responsibility for children, and build on valuable aspects of colonial heritage."

That was the distilled summary of what I had learnt, fitted into the Twitter format, and conveyed in four tweets.

Of course it brought out the usual army of trolls and twirritants who replied that South Africa would be better off if all whites left the country, and other inane nonsense. I shrugged.

I should have left it at that.

My key mistake is always assuming people are, at root, reasonable, fair, and rational. And that every no-hoper warrants a response.

So, I replied:

"For those claiming legacy of colonialism was ONLY negative, think of our independent judiciary, transport infrastructure, piped water etc."

That was the tweet that nearly ended my political life. Looking back on the original, I now see it garnered a mere 1,000 comments (a combination of support and criticism), 464 retweets and 500 likes. With a million followers, it was actually a non-event.

Except that Eusebius McKaiser and his support base in the DA managed to turn it into Hiroshima.

The first time I realised that a slow motion nuclear explosion was underway was when Geordin Hill-Lewis, Mmusi Maimane's Chief of Staff, phoned me while we were still on the tarmac on the final leg of our trip, the flight from Johannesburg to Cape Town.

I could immediately hear the edge in his voice.

"Just apologise." he said, "Apologise and withdraw."

"Apologise for what?" I asked.

I was genuinely puzzled.

"Your tweet." he said in exasperation.

"Which one?" I asked.

"The one about the legacy of colonialism not being only negative," he answered.

"What?" I asked, totally incredulous.

Geordin went on to explain that DA parliamentarians were in the midst of their weekly Thursday caucus meeting when their Twitter feeds had started bubbling, sending the Woke undercurrents in the DA's own caucus on the boil.

"There is absolutely nothing wrong with what I said. I was not defending or justifying colonialism. I just said its legacy is not *only* negative.

That is what I learnt in Singapore, and I put it in that context. To interpret it any other way is pure distortion and manipulation.

It is an attempt to close down an uncomfortable conversation before it begins," I fumed.

"What's more, South Africa needs to have this conversation. Why should I be barred, as Premier of the Western Cape, from speaking about the valuable lessons I learnt in Singapore?"

I had gone to Singapore as premier and I was sharing the learnings as premier, I told him. I had no role at all anymore in the DA's internal leadership structures.

By that time, we had reached the plane and I couldn't continue talking. Nor could Geordin.

"For goodness' sake, just apologise," he repeated.

"Mmusi is under pressure and you have to help him deal with it."

"This is utterly ridiculous." I said before ringing off, "Surely we can still have adult conversations in South Africa?"

This, of course, was a rhetorical question. I knew we couldn't. We are fundamentally incapable in this respect. I was back home.

So, before I got onto the plane, I made my first mistake by tweeting:

"I apologise unreservedly for a tweet that may have come across as a defence of colonialism. It was not."

Interestingly, by way of comparison with my offending tweet, my apology got 427 likes, 1,695 retweets and 1,267 comments.

More people had "liked" my original tweet than the apology. But more than three times the number of people retweeted my apology. I am sure they were friendly souls who presumed that my apology would bring an end to this Hiroshima in a handbasket.

Of course it didn't.

Unsurprisingly, Eusebius McKaiser led the way in performative outrage, by rejecting my apology. He wanted to take the "scandal" to the next level.

"No Helen No. It didn't 'come across as a defence of Colonialism'. IT WAS A DEFENCE. What a sheepish non-apology. You simply were yourself," he raged (being entirely himself).

This was just one of 26 tweets and retweets Eusebius fired off in rapid succession in the space of two hours.

His producer made almost as many phone calls to Mmusi, pressuring him into coming onto Eusebius' talk show on 702.

When Mmusi eventually relented, Eusebius (a former World Debating Champion, as he is wont to remind us) bludgeoned Mmusi into a corner, forcing him to concede I was "bigoted". After that, Eusebius conducted his chorus of callers to a fitting crescendo.

All this was happening while I was safely cocooned at 37,000 feet above sea level between Johannesburg and Cape Town, safe from Twitter's reach. By the time I landed, there was blood and guts everywhere.

I arrived at the office in time to get a quick briefing before going to the Premier's Portfolio Committee to answer questions on our annual report. My staff were ashen-faced.

Unlike Chris Hart, however, I was spared the deep freeze treatment. My colleagues supported me through thick and thin. But they were worried.

I tried to reassure them. Quoting Bill Clinton speaking to his aides as the Monica Lewinsky scandal broke, I said: "This is going to be messy, but survivable."

They were not so sure.

I was profoundly irritated: "South Africa is going to have to grow up and have these conversations. But perhaps we prefer wandering blindfolded down Zimbabwe's dead-end of decolonising everything, including our currency." I had recently read an article about how poor Zimbabweans had been paying school fees in chickens and goats.

"Don't tweet that," they warned me. There was always humour in that office, even in the darkest hole.

My two closest colleagues in the party had always been Gavin Davis and Geordin Hill-Lewis. Both were MPs and Geordin filled the post of Mmusi's Chief of Staff too.

They thought the issue would blow over in a week following my tweeted apology. Looking back, I disagree with this view, having learnt from numerous similar examples that apologising in the face of a howling mob when you have done nothing wrong merely deepens the hole you are in.

But, apart from my apology, there was an intervening event in the course of that week that changed the trajectory. It was the deadline for my regular column in the *Daily Maverick*. Both the editor, Brank Brkic, and I agreed that there was no other topic I could write on that week but the furore unleashed by my tweeted commentary on the Singapore trip.

Rereading the article I wrote titled "Lessons from Singapore", it is clear that I understood a major *Zeitgeist* shift was in progress, and that I was very worried about its impact on the DA and on South Africa.

I ended the article with the following observation:

"The real danger is that the DA, in its quest for votes, may start to swallow every tenet, myth and shibboleth of African racial-nationalist propaganda, including the scapegoating of minorities, populist mobilisation and political patronage. Then the institutionalisation of corruption will only be a matter of time.

"If this were to happen, it will be irrelevant whether we win or lose elections, because we will no longer offer an alternative. That is why these debates are not a diversion. It is essential to have them."

I learnt later that these final paragraphs of my article, sincerely meant and deeply felt, had been regarded as a declaration of war by the DA leadership. Paul Boughey (the DA's Chief Executive Officer), Jonathan Moakes (the Chief Strategist) and James Selfe (Chair of Federal Council) resolved that I had to go. Mmusi, as always, was on the fence.

Geordin and Gavin tried to prevent the escalating conflict. They knew I was prepared to fight the matter all the way to the Constitutional Court, on principle. And they wanted to prevent a protracted and very public political fallout.

I wanted to bring the DA to its senses.

The three of us wanted the best for the party but we were following divergent pathways in a political labyrinth, from different vantage points.

The issue grew legs and ran for weeks. Every columnist and *nochschlepper* piled in, except interestingly, the ANC leadership. They said not a word.

Maybe they thought I had made a necessary point in the middle of the "decolonisation" fracas. Or maybe they just let Bell Pottinger do their work for them.

Nonetheless, the DA leadership wanted me out.

But if they thought I was going to buckle, they were wrong. Applying Newton's first law of motion, I ensured that for every irrational attack, there was an equal and opposite response, where I stated my case as dispassionately as I could.

Geordin and Gavin were convinced that the looming battle would only have one result: Mutually Assured Destruction. But, instinctively, both they and I knew the DA had no case against me.

The party leadership tried everything possible to get me to buckle. One involved the convening of a "Debate of Urgent Public Importance" in the Provincial Legislature. I laugh when I think that over my ten years as head of government in the Western Cape, this was the only debate of urgent public importance that the Speaker convened — to discuss a 140-character tweet stating the bleeding obvious.

I welcomed the opportunity to defend my statement.

In my speech to the Legislature, I quoted Nelson Mandela and the contemporary Grade 12 history textbook to underscore my points. Both had made exactly the same point, only more forcefully and unambiguously than I had.

Predictably, this did not mollify the DA leadership one bit. They suspended me from the party without going through the constitutionally defined process. In fact, I first heard the news that I had been suspended on my car radio while travelling back from a DA event in Mitchell's Plain where I had been the guest speaker.

Next, the DA handed me a charge sheet as long as my arm, with an instruction to appear before the party's Federal Legal Commission for violating the DA's Constitution and social media policy.

In preparation for the inquisition, I commissioned two separate legal opinions which both gave me the same advice: You didn't violate the DA's Constitution; you didn't violate any of the DA's policies. You may have caused offence — but everything the DA ever says causes offence to someone. Causing offence is the very nature of politics. If causing offence is turned into an offence by the DA, it cannot operate as a political party.

"There is no case against you. If you lose in the DA's internal systems, you will win in the courts."

My lawyers then asked the DA for "further particulars" including all the polling on which the charges were based. The DA was profoundly reluctant to give me this "confidential information." It was only years later that I was to learn why.

My preparation for my hearing included the appointment of a forensic IT expert to draw links between the Twitter posts and establish how the "influencers" were interconnected, with the purpose of maximising the online outrage. I was ready.

The DA's lawyers must have been giving the party the same advice about the weakness of their case, because they suddenly became more amenable to Geordin's and Gavin's advice to find a way to settle the escalating conflict.

The two came to see me. By then, the relationship between us had become somewhat strained. They were trying to straddle what seemed an unbridgeable divide.

I was cooking supper in the cool, soothing black-and-white tiled kitchen at Leeuwenhof, the premier's residence.

The three of us remember the conversation that unfolded differently — but the bottom line of their quest was to find some sort of compromise that would prevent further escalation.

After the initial skirmishes, they cut to the chase.

"Look, the DA knows it is going to lose this case. If you win, it will be the end of Mmusi."

"He picked this fight, not me," I responded, frying onions.

Looking back, it is clear that I had not grasped the full extent of the madness that had gripped the party.

I only realised it when Geordin and Gavin explained that this internal "fight to the death" between the current leader and the former leader had been escalated as a *deliberate strategy.*

The purpose, they said, was to engineer a "catalytic moment" in which Mmusi would emerge victorious, with my head on a platter, to prove that the DA was no longer a "white party". It would enable him to establish his uncontested leadership and rid himself once and for all of the "puppet" tag.

Geordin and Gavin thought this strategy would tear the party apart, and were doing their best to prevent it careening towards inexorable disaster.

I just thought the very notion was absurd. I had spent my entire leadership trying to prove that the DA was a party for everyone who believed in non-racialism, constitutionalism, a market economy, and competent governance.

I had supported internal racial transformation to the point where 8 out of 9 provincial leaders were black, and had stepped back myself to make way for a black leader.

And none of that had done anything to change the narrative of the DA being a white party.

Nor would it change if Mmusi ousted me. The reason was simple. The ANC has no other argument except race. They cannot point to a single one of their policies that has worked in practice. They cannot point to a single place they govern properly, so all they can do is revert to race.

"The facts are irrelevant," I said. "Any black leader of the DA will always be described as a 'white puppet'— in just the same way that Zanu-PF continues to accuse its opposition of being puppets of the British in Zimbabwe. This is not going to change by getting rid of me."

I sensed that Geordin and Gavin agreed with me, but they were trying to increase the pressure on me to succumb to a settlement — which would involve a second apology.

They pressed on. "If you continue through this hearing, and win in court, that is the end of Mmusi, and it will do the party massive — probably irreparable — damage. He will be seen to have taken you on and lost. He will not recover from that. And if this battle drags on through the courts for three years, nor will the party."

That argument made sense to me.

It took a couple of days but eventually they convinced me to acquiesce to a public humiliation, in order to help Mmusi out of his corner and bring the DA's bleeding to an end.

I would have to apologise again and be publicly reprimanded before the entire assembled press corps at a staged event in Johannesburg.

The hypocrisy of the whole thing was nauseating. If the DA leadership had been prepared to follow through on the battle they had started, I would have won.

But, once they realised they had to back out of it, I had to help them do it in the interests of the party.

I had offered a first apology, in the tweet from the O R Tambo tarmac, to help Mmusi out of a corner, and he promptly painted himself into another one.

Now we had to go through the same movie again, only this time in 3D Cinerama.

When I learnt of the political strategy Mmusi was following, I realised he would never run out of corners to paint himself into.

He was operating inside a self-constructed metaphorical rhombicosidodecahedron, which has the most corners of any known geometric structure, with 20 regular triangular faces, 30 square faces, and 12 regular pentagonal faces.

I knew he and his inner circle would run out of credibility long before they ran out of corners.

But back to the presser in the Hilton Hotel in Rosebank.

I will never forget Mmusi's face, haughty as Herod, as we walked into the packed press conference.

I knew I had to get through the next hour by keeping my mind active and distracted.

As Mmusi's speech passed in a blur of words, I imagined myself in the Monty Python movie *Life of Brian* as the man condemned to death by stoning, for violating a speech code of the ancient Hebrews.

He had sinned by telling his wife her halibut recipe was so good, it was befitting of "Jehovah".

For taking the Lord's name in vain he deserved to die. The blood-thirsty crowd lined up with handfuls of stones, waiting for the high priest, brilliantly played by John Cleese, to blow his whistle so that they could let rip and flatten the blasphemer.

I didn't yet understand that Wokeness had reintroduced pre-Enlightenment conventions for dealing with dissenters.

But the brilliant twist of that Monty Python skit is that the biggest stone fells the high priest first.

That was a perfect metaphor for what happened on that stage.

There were, in truth, no winners.

But perhaps mutually assured humiliation was preferable to mutually assured destruction.

Despite the public performance, little changed as far as my rela-tionship with the DA was concerned. Although the charges were dropped to prevent the spectacle of me winning in court, I remained suspended from all party activities.

Behind the scenes, Paul Boughey and Jonathan Moakes continued the pressure to have me fired — despite the agreement and the staged apology.

They presented a detailed written strategy to the DA's Federal Executive arguing that I should be sent to a university abroad with immediate effect, and that the DA's most effective parliamentarians should have their volume turned down — because they were white.

It was an electoral suicide note posing as a plan to save South Africa.

I just ignored the rambling mess of contradictions, and hung in there.

My suspension from political activities turned out to be a blessing in disguise because it gave me my weekends back. During this precious time, I could bond with my first grand-child, named Mila to honour the memory of my beloved mother.

I was, for the first time, relieved that my mother had died before she could meet her first great-grandchild, because her death also spared her from witnessing the DA leadership's attempts to crush me. She had always opposed my going into politics, and this spectacle would have destroyed her.

The "cancelling" was not confined to the DA. I had some moments of amusement at the types of people that jumped on the bandwagon to parade their Woke credentials.

Take Shelagh Foster, director of the Franschhoek Literary Festival.

It must have slipped her mind that the written word (and the English language) are part of colonialism's legacy in South Africa. She didn't skip a beat in decontextualizing, distorting, and catastrophizing what I had said, as she "pulled me from the programme" of the 2017 Festival.

Full of indignant self-righteousness, she wrote to the publisher of my autobiography that I was no longer welcome: "We enjoy controversy but not of this nature. Please could you inform her private secretary."

Next to cancel me was the Kingsmead Book Fair, scheduled for May 2017. I quote the letter written by the festival director to my office manager, Donnae Strydom, in full:

From: Hayley Pienaar [mailto:hpienaar@kingsmead.co.za]

Sent: Wednesday, March 22, 2017 2:17 PM

To: Donnae Strydom <Donnae.Strydom@westerncape.gov.za>

Cc: Lisa Kaplan <lkaplan@kingsmead.co.za>; Ann Leith <aleith@kingsmead.co.za>; Carol Eedes <carol@alphabettravel.co.za>; Ellen Van Schalkwyk <EvanSchalkwyk@penguinrandomhouse.co.za>

Subject: Kingsmead Book Fair Saturday 13 May

Importance: High

Dear Donnae

On behalf of the Kingsmead Book Fair, we regret to inform you that there has been an overwhelming call from our various stakeholders to withdraw Helen Zille from the Kingsmead Book Fair programme. Hence, we trust that you will understand our decision to withdraw her accordingly.

We apologise for any inconvenience this may cause.

Thank you for your understanding.

Courage Always

Hayley

Read that carefully and look at the sign-off line: "Courage Always". That gave me a belly laugh. Organisers of a book fair incapable of recognising irony!

And then, the cherry on the top eighteen months later, was being cancelled by my own alma mater, St Mary's School for Girls in Waverley, Johannesburg. The year 2018 was the 50th Reunion of our 1968 graduating year, and a few of us were really looking forward to meeting up again and reminiscing.

I was nominated by the organising committee to read a passage from the Bible on behalf of the Old Girls at the chapel service that was to be part of the programme.

A few days before the event, Deanne King, the head of school (the person we used to call the headmistress) called me and asked me to withdraw from the programme. Why, I asked, dumbfounded.

"Because some of the Grade 12s are planning a protest if you don't," she replied.

A little further probing revealed that it was because of my tweet saying the legacy of colonialism was not *only* negative.

What? Here are girls whose parents have chosen to send them to a school that epitomises just about every aspect of colonialism's legacy, wanting to "de-platform" me from doing a Bible reading in an Anglican chapel. Did they need reminding that Christianity in South Africa (and specifically Anglicanism) is yet another legacy of colonialism?

I told the "head of school" it was time for her to grow a backbone. She was withdrawing me from the programme because a handful of offended girls were going to stage a hollow protest against a distorted and decontextualized version of my observations on returning from Singapore.

Frankly, I should never have expected anything more from St Mary's. They have never encountered a hierarchical power system that they did not genuflect to.

There is a famous saying in politics: "People worship the rising sun, not the setting sun."

I was definitely the setting sun, and I expected to be abandoned, like an old elephant pushed out of the herd.

But I was sincerely amazed at how many people stood by me, against their own interests, which is extremely rare in life, let alone in politics.

My cabinet and caucus in the Western Cape government never flinched in their support, despite the daily onslaught from the DA's Federal Head Office attempting to get them to turn against me. They remained resolute.

And then there was Ashor Sarupen, an MPL in the Gauteng Provincial Legislature. One of the smartest and most principled people in politics today, Ashor took his political life in his hands by openly supporting me. He came to my office to give me the full background of the strategy to oust me. And he told the party they were behaving like authoritarian idiots.

In return, one of the party's senior leaders told him that his support of me would be "career suicide".

"That's fine," Ashor replied, "but I have a conscience to live with."

Geordin and Gavin were in impossible positions, trying to straddle the canyon between the DA strategists and myself in the search for some sort of compromise to end the stand-off. They were putting as much pressure on the party's leadership as they were on me. That took courage — at both ends.

And so the months in Purgatory dragged on, until in mid-2018, something quite unexpected happened.

Twitter had its first major "bot-cull". Overnight, on 12 July 2018, my Twitter following dropped by over 25,000.

I learnt from the *Washington Post* that the abuse of fake accounts had become so prevalent, and used for such nefarious purposes, that this practice was threatening Twitter's credibility and financial model as a social media platform.

So, Twitter developed new algorithms to identify the most malevolent fake accounts, and deleted them. Not all fake accounts, mind you. Just the most egregious ones.

But when I learnt how many of the most vicious accounts were active on my timeline, I immediately saw the opportunity to identify the extent to which these fake accounts had been involved in manufacturing the outrage over my "legacy of colonialism" tweet the previous year.

So, I went back to my forensic IT expert. He agreed that we had a unique opportunity to quantify the presence of malicious bot accounts in the historical datasets around the controversy. He thought it best to focus on March 16 and 17, 2017 when the hysteria around my tweets had begun and had rapidly reached fever pitch.

In his final written report, he set the context:

"It is worth noting," he wrote, "that a few accounts can have an out-sized impact. For example, ~3,000 accounts associated with the Russian Internet Research Agency (IRA) are credited with playing an important role in swinging the 2016 USA elections away from Hillary Clinton to Donald Trump."

Similarly, in South Africa, it had been established that a mere 800 fake accounts linked to the Gupta network were responsible for creating the entire online narrative around Economic Apartheid, White Monopoly Capital (WMC) and Radical Economic Transformation (RET).

It was therefore fascinating to discover the extent of the activity of fake accounts and botnets on my own timeline. The key facts are as follows:

Of the accounts amplifying the furore around my tweet(s) during the first two days on 16 and 17 March 2017, 2,025 accounts were subsequently suspended by Twitter. We could safely conclude that they had been removed through Twitter's bot-cull.

Another 4,885 accounts had been deleted or renamed by their owners.

In the course of those two days, the combination of suspended and deleted accounts was involved in authoring or amplifying 21,000 hostile tweets on my timeline.

The 2,025 suspended users generated 4,296 tweets — 73% of which were retweets for amplification and 27% of which were original tweets.

The 4,885 deleted and renamed users generated 17,135 tweets.

Interestingly, my consultant specifically identified an account named @adamitv as being central to the outrage manufacturing machine during this period, not only in my case, but also in several others.

Some rudimentary research revealed that @adamitv is Dr Mohamed Adam, a medical alumnus of the University of the Witwatersrand. He has over 300 companies registered in his name, and obviously the question arose: What does he use them all for? The South African Revenue Service may want to take a look.

He lists himself as chairman of Louis Pasteur Holdings, and it was interesting to learn that Louis Pasteur Hospital Holdings had, just one year after its chairman's efforts to destroy me online, lost a R44 million court action in which the Supreme Court of Appeal had rejected the company's evidence outright, saying it could not be relied upon.

Mohamed is also Chairman of the ITV Foundation in South Africa, about which there is scant information online. So, @Adamitv is himself a real person.

However, he now runs his account under the name @Adamitv-RSS. This account shows no posts after 2015, but he clearly updated his profile after 2017. Did he perhaps delete his more recent posts to cover his tracks as the net closed on the network of bots in which he had played such a key role?

His profile explains that "the @Adamitv main account has been blocked by Twitter. No reason given."

I'll give you the reason, @Adamitv. For free. It is because you, Dr Mohamed Adam, were central to the Guptabot network, working both for them and against me. You authored tweets and then amplified them using bots sourced from the international market. Twitter identified what you were doing and therefore erased your main account. Stop feigning ignorance. You know enough about IT to understand why your account was suspended.

It is people like you, @Adamitv, who helped destroy what could have been the most valuable platform for democratic, rational, and open debate. Purposefully.

I now had all the empirical evidence I needed to show just how much the outcry had been digitally manipulated, and dramatically boosted by real people in the DA, in particular (as my research revealed) several DA public representatives, cheered on by Eusebius McKaiser.

But, over a year later, when I had gathered all this information, there was no point in picking open an old sore.

I knew I would be able to use it one day, so I simply stored it in a file I called "*Skietgoed*" (fire power).

Anyway, by that time, the party's fight with me was old news. The DA, following the incomprehensible strategy of picking fights with its top vote-winners, was now trying its best to demolish the Mayor of Cape Town, Patricia de Lille.

There may have been valid complaints against Patricia — but there is only one legal way of getting rid of a mayor and that is through a vote of no-confidence. Having failed in this attempt, the DA tried every other trick in the book to get around the law, each of which left more egg on its face.

Patricia had also backed Mmusi into a corner, but there was no way she was letting him slither his way out of it. She took him on and won in court at least three times in the run-up to the 2019 election.

What's more, the DA, inexplicably, continued to scour social media for racially divisive narratives, and joined the online battle from a perspective of identity politics — assuming whites to be the villains.

So, it came as no surprise when out of the blue, I received a call from a senior campaign manager saying, quite predictably, that the party's polling showed us shedding support hand-over-fist. Would I be prepared to go out and campaign for the DA in Gauteng and the Eastern and Western Cape?

"Sure," I said. And, although I was still formally suspended from all party activities, I threw myself heart and soul into shoring up our support in these heartland provinces.

Some of my colleagues and family asked me why I was doing this, after the way the party had treated me. I told them the future of the country could not be derailed by hurt feelings.

"If we don't have the DA, we have nothing between South Africa and Zimbabwe. If the DA fails, South Africa fails. We went through a bad patch. All organisations and individuals do. It is part of life. It's the resilience that matters. We will recover, and part of that recovery involves canvassing to retain as much support as possible."

Mmusi continued to ignore me, even as I slogged day and night to help bring in the vote that he and his "strategic advisers" had so successfully alienated from the party. In fact, I have always thought it something of an irony that, during my leadership, I brought three times more new black voters to the DA than Mmusi ever did.

But the fallout from the internalisation of Wokeness by some in the DA was not quite over yet.

After our humiliating 2019 election result, I made a last-minute decision to run for the position of the DA's Federal Council to replace James Selfe. I could understand why Mmusi was filled with trepidation. His chosen candidate was Athol Trollip, and he threw everything into the battle to get him elected.

My victory must have come as a shock, but I was prepared to work with him again, and put the past behind us. I phoned him and told him as much. I meant it sincerely.

Preparing for my first Federal Executive meeting a week after my election, I phoned Mmusi twice, and he seemed cordial and professional. I asked to meet him two hours before the meeting to go through the agenda and ensure he was happy with what I had prepared. He agreed.

As I sat opposite him on that Wednesday morning, he seemed agitated and uncomfortable, but we went through the agenda, and I again committed to working with him towards an early Congress.

He seemed to agree. But as I should have known, his greatest skill — dissembling — was on full display. I do not think he was being deliberately devious. I just think he lacked the courage to be honest. Corners were his comfort zone.

During the course of chairing my first Fedex meeting later that morning, tensions rose. Athol, equally wounded at the election result, led the attack. I sought to bring the meeting back on course, until I realised there was something else going on. A plan was unfolding, but I couldn't quite fathom what it was.

Then I got a Whatsapp message from my son in Cape Town.

"I'm sorry things are turning out this way, Ma," the message read.

"What do you mean?" I replied.

"That Mmusi is resigning and blaming you."

"What?" I replied puzzled, "I am sitting right next to him in a meeting. I had a two-hour private meeting with him this morning and I know nothing about this at all."

"Social media is full of Mmusi's resignation," replied my son.

There and then, I stopped the meeting in its tracks.

"Is there perhaps something you should be telling us," I asked Mmusi and Athol.

After a bit more ducking and diving I said directly: "I have just received a Whatsapp telling me you are about to resign and that you will blame that decision on me. Is that correct?"

I wanted a yes or no answer.

Neither Mmusi nor Athol could dodge it any longer. They conceded that their plan was, at the lunch break, to go downstairs and announce to the assembled press corps in the media room that they were resigning.

One by one, the Fedex argued that this move was unnecessary. That they should give it a try. They asked for a break to caucus, but by that time, with the press corps downstairs and well briefed, it was too late. They could not change their mind and escape the corner they had created for themselves.

I, and several others, had been completely blind-sided.

The rest of the afternoon passed in a haze.

I had had enough. If anyone had reason to be offended over what had transpired over the past few years, it was I. Yet, here they were acting as if they were the victims. But I kept a straight face, looking appropriately serious, and got through yet another media fracas.

Predictably and true to form, in his final speech, Mmusi painted himself into his final DA corner. He announced that he did not regard the DA as the "appropriate vehicle" to build "one South Africa for all".

Following this declaration, he said he was resigning as DA leader, but intended staying on as the parliamentary leader.

Say what?

Did he really believe he could announce that the party was no longer an appropriate vehicle to achieve a common nationhood in South Africa, and in the same breath claim the right to continue as the DA's parliamentary leader — and in that capacity, as Leader of the Opposition?

This time, no one intended giving Mmusi a free pass out of his umpteenth corner.

The very next day, a motion of no confidence was tabled against him in the parliamentary caucus. Mmusi resigned before having to face the indignity of being drummed out of that office.

Of course the press lapped it up. Having pilloried Mmusi throughout his leadership of the "white party" and labelling him a "puppet", his departure from the DA instantly transformed him into the victim-hero, vanquished by the forces of Whiteness.

I was the white Mephistopheles, the crafty demon whose sin was to have stood for a democratic election, campaigned fairly and won convincingly. That's Whiteness for you!

It took me a couple of months to feel my way into a new job that is aptly described as the DA's toilet cleaner. And some of the toilets had clearly not been flushed for a while.

Some of the things I hauled out of the sewers were pretty smelly.

Let me mention just one example that is relevant to my account of the politics of personal destruction.

The DA had set up an investigation into various incidents and events that the party believed may have contributed to our disappointing 2019 election result.

One of these was my tweet on the legacy of colonialism.

Refiloe Nt'sekhe, who was heading the investigation, requested me to make a submission on my analysis of the incident and its aftermath. Others involved in the matter were offered the same opportunity.

The key question that Refiloe had to answer was this: did my tweet cost the DA votes? After the furore surrounding it, I assumed there would have been a high cost, but I was interested in finding out just how much.

According to the charge sheet which the Federal Legal Commission (FLC) had drawn up against me, it appeared as if I had done profound damage.

So, in preparing my own submission, I requested access to the DA's polling data on the matter.

With the permission of the FLC, I undertook an analysis of the research, with the assistance of the DA's Chief Research Officer Johan van der Berg.

This detailed analysis revealed that almost every allegation in the charge sheet that claimed to reflect the DA's polling, was actually a blatant misrepresentation of the polling conducted by the DA between March 27 and March 30 — on which the charge sheet against me was based.

In this poll, as is the DA's standard practice in conducting nuanced quantitative research, a number of statements were put to respondents who were asked whether they agreed or disagreed with them. The poll found:

1. 57% of black voters *agreed* with the statement that "the legacy of colonialism was not only negative, but also positive". In other words, a significant majority of black voters actually *supported* the wording of my tweet, with the addition of the word "positive" as applied to the legacy of colonialism (a description I had never used).

2. 54% of black voters *agreed* with the statement that South Africa "could not have developed without being colonised". In other words, a majority of black voters actually went *further* than what I had said in my tweet, and said South Africa could not have developed without

being colonised. I had never said any such thing, but the answer to the question underscored the answers to the first, reinforcing the reliability of the finding.

3. Fully 38% of black voters said that my tweets would actually make them *more likely* to vote DA. This is the most extraordinary result of all, given that the most we have ever polled in an election is 6% among black voters. To have 38% of black voters polled in a random stratified sample saying that my tweet made them more likely to vote DA showed me that the tweet actually had a net positive impact on voting intention.

In other words, there was no quantitative evidence whatsoever in the poll conducted between the dates specified in the charge sheet to substantiate the charges. Quite the contrary. No wonder the DA didn't want to hand over the results of the polling to my lawyers back in 2017.

The lesson we need to learn from this is simple: although the Wokes make a disproportionate amount of noise, they do not speak for most people. Instead, they use online terror tactics to vilify and cancel people with different opinions, drive them off social media, and eventually out of their jobs.

But, as it took us a while to learn, Twitter is not the Voters' Roll.

The DA learned the hard way that when we followed the Woke narrative, we actually lost votes.

There was also little doubt, and very clear quantitative evidence, that the DA's conscious strategy of picking fights with me and Patricia de Lille had done far more damage to the party than any of our alleged transgressions.

I asked the FLC who had provided the data contained in the charge sheet. The answer was Jonathan Moakes. Johan reported to Jonathan. I asked Johan how this was possible. He said he had no knowledge of the specifics of what Jonathan was feeding through to the Federal Legal Commission, or the Federal Executive or the Federal Council.

Then Johan concluded: "It is clear they wanted to use polling to support the drive to get you out, but the polling didn't support their position, so they had to manipulate the results."

I thought Paul Boughey and Jonathan Moakes were capable of many things, but manipulating polling data was a step that I did not think they would be capable of.

As a result, one of the first reforms I introduced as Chairperson of the Federal Council was to make sure that the polling function of the party was separated from the strategic function.

Johan himself now reports directly to Federal Council and Federal Executive on the polling results, without any intermediaries, so that we can interrogate the facts, not the twisted self-serving versions served up by those who devise failing strategies.

It is far too tempting for strategists to manipulate polling data to fit their strategy rather than to use polling data to inform their strategy. That is why the separation of these functions is essential.

So why, given what I have described above, should anyone vote for the DA?

The reason is that we are the only party that digs to the root of our problems, eradicates the rot, and nurtures the plant back to health.

And the rot had not yet gone deep enough to threaten our survival. We were able to cut out the cancer and recover relatively fast.

In the end, all of us in the DA are human. We make mistakes. I am personally responsible for one of the biggest mistakes in the DA's history, which was supporting Mmusi's candidature for the leadership. But we learnt from our mistakes and we are fixing them.

That is one reason that we should vote for the DA.

The second is that we are the only party in South Africa that stands unequivocally for non-racialism and constitutionalism, and a policy package that will enable South Africa to succeed.

If there is one party that knows exactly how destructive racialised ideologies like Wokeness truly are, it is the DA. We have lived through its impact, and I am grateful that we have survived to tell the tale.

Ironic as it may sound, I also believe that we are stronger for having gone through a period where the party's top leadership flirted with the notion of dumping the DA's foundational commitment to liberal non-racialism.

Today, the DA is more deeply and resolutely committed to our core values than we have been in many years. It is precisely because we have all witnessed the devastation and decline occasioned by racialised politics up-close, that we are determined never to make the same painful mistakes again.

As the Progressive Party's founding leader, Jannie Steytler said in the early 1960s: "One day South Africa *will* be governed by our values because it is the only way it *can* be governed."

That statement remains as true today as it was sixty years ago. And it will still be true in another 60 years' time.

Each of us must run our allotted portion of the race before passing on the baton.

I thought my time had come, back in 2015, when I stepped down as leader, but when the DA went so badly off course due to the capitulation before Wokeness, I felt I had to return. I had to help fix the mess I had helped to create.

The next chapter seeks to explain why.

7

Why SA Won't Survive
Wokeness

THIS CHAPTER IDENTIFIES ten of the most important reasons why entrenching Wokeness — the politics of racial and gender identity — will be South Africa's death knell, unless we can counter it successfully.

My focus here is primarily on the politics of racial identity, because this is South Africa's overriding form of Wokeness. Other types are a present and growing reality, but are all currently subordinate to the overwhelming weight of race.

The purpose of this chapter is to assist people who wish to marshal effective counter arguments.

Although the word "Woke" is a relatively recent arrival on our shores, driven here on the wave of American cultural imperialism through the internet, the ideology that underpins Wokeness is not new to our country.

The ANC may not formally use the term, but its policies were Woke before anyone in South Africa had ever heard of the word (despite its hypocritical rhetorical commitment to non-racialism).

And so it was with the National Party. Apartheid was premised precisely on the "woke" idea that a person should be judged by the colour of their skin, not the content of their character.

The Woke generation, who never lived through apartheid's racial engineering, would probably be highly offended to learn that they have embraced the policies of race classification and racial preferencing that lay at the heart of the system they claim to despise.

They may also be surprised to realise that the ANC seamlessly picked up where apartheid left off, merely switching the melanin count of the beneficiaries. And, based on numerical superiority, the ANC's election strategy since 1994 has focused primarily on race mobilisation.

Applied to South African demographics, this strategy — which nullifies the principle of non-racialism — makes minorities feel impotent to effect real change through the ballot box. If race mobilisation makes it impossible to change one's government by voting, minorities become effectively disenfranchised.

This is the key reason for the recent growth in secessionist movements in areas of South Africa where "minorities" working together can constitute an electoral majority.

The tragic irony is that the Woke Wave from America hit us just as the spectacular failure of the ANC's policies of racial engineering became so glaringly apparent, through a dysfunctional state, a collapsing economy, and 12 million unemployed job-seekers.

But for many young people who live online, the algorithms of Google and Facebook prevent them from grasping the significance of this. They are trapped in a digital echo chamber where they are fed content by the tech giants, designed to reinforce their prejudices and predilections. Connectivity has served to narrow, rather than broaden, their worldview.

It is not uncommon these days for young South Africans to know all about political developments in the United States (through a woke prism), but absolutely nothing about events in their own country — even when these events are as shocking as the revelations about State Security slush funds being used by the ANC to buy off judges and journalists to support the ruling party.

Whatever the confluence of reasons, we have failed to learn the lessons of our own recent history. We have also failed to understand their implications. Otherwise we would, by now, be truly committed to non-racialism.

But the contrary is true. "Racial transformation" has become the ANC's overriding policy imperative, not just one of several policy goals. The purpose of this focus, when one cuts through the hollow rhetoric, was to legalise corruption and enable the politically-connected to burrow into every capital flow in the country, in order to loot.

They pretended the goal was "broad-based black economic empowerment". Anyone who ever believed that must surely, by now, realise they were conned.

Of course, colonialism and apartheid played the primary role in the structural exclusion of black South Africans from the political economy. That is a fact, and we have to redress that profound injustice.

But Wokeness and the re-racialisation of South Africa's political economy is not the way to do it.

The list of ten reasons backing up this categorical statement is not exhaustive. Neither is the list in priority order. It is merely in a sequence that makes logical sense. It is the combination of these factors that is killing South Africa's prospects.

1. Wokeness is an exercise in self-deception and misdiagnosis.

It claims that "Whiteness" is the core problem in South Africa. For the vast majority of people, this translates into the conclusion that whites are the core problem in South Africa, and have been since Jan van Riebeeck first put his foot on solid ground on the Southern tip of Africa in 1652. The corollary of this idea is that salvation lies in the removal of whites from all positions of power and authority, and for some, from the country as well.

Until that happens, the logic continues, South Africa will remain divided into two main groups: The Villains (comprising about 8% of South Africa's population) vs. Everyone Else.

This simplistic diagnosis, an article of faith for South African Wokeness, is a massive barrier to addressing the real problems our country faces. It also prevents us from building a successful, inclusive future.

Wokeness has given the ANC the courage to reveal its true nature as a black nationalist organisation. Its commitment to non-racialism and independent institutions of state was always paper thin — a temporary compromise to move the country through the "first stage" of the bourgeois revolution, with the backing of Western powers, before moving onto the second stage.

On the 5th March 2012, the policy sub-committee of the ANC's National Executive Committee announced the commencement of the "second stage", seeking to bring the "National Democratic Revolution" (NDR) to its conclusion. Its fulfilment will mean the party will control the State and all its institutions; and the State will control the economy and society.

Jacob Zuma, president at the time, promised that "Radical Economic Transformation" imposed through all institutions of State, would eradicate the imaginary bogeyman "White Monopoly Capital".

Before the transition to democracy, the ANC was always quite open about its intentions. As late as 1998, its policy guru Joel Netshitenzhe, who was later to become the head of the policy and coordination advisory unit in the presidency, wrote in the ANC mouthpiece that the aim of the NDR "is extending the power of the 'National Liberation Movement' over all levers of power: the army, the police, the bureaucracy, intelligence structures, the judiciary, parastatals, and agencies such as regulatory bodies, the public broadcaster, the central bank and so on".

Enter Wokeness, 15 years later, to provide a perfect "moral" cover for rolling out the next stage of this plan, complete with a new lexicon, for its long-term trajectory.

While the National Party focused on the "displacement of blackness" from "white" South Africa, the Woke movement — which has a growing grip on the ruling ANC — focuses on the vanquishing of "whiteness".

Both the ANC and the NP have in common their sense of a historic mission to redeem their people (racially defined) from oppression and subjugation. They are, in truth, two sides of the same historical coin. And both will leave equally dark stains on South Africa's history.

2. Wokeness encourages victimhood and destroys agency.

Victimhood is the most disabling and disempowering psychological state there is, because victims, by definition, can do very little about their circumstances. Victimhood destroys personal agency — which is the key driver of social progress. Victims depend on the favour of their persecutors, the Villains, to advance in life.

The notion that whites, and white male heterosexuals in particular, are all-powerful to determine the life chances of others, is actually a racist and sexist notion that imbues a group, by biological definition, with supreme control to determine the destiny of others. If white heterosexual males are the puppet-masters, everyone else is, by extension, a puppet.

The implications of that assumption are devastating for development.

While it is true that millions of people lack the capabilities or means to transform their life circumstances (and in that sense they can be described as "victims"), an exclusive focus on blaming "villains" (racially defined) distracts us from dealing with the real causes of poverty and economic exclusion.

In fact, it merely serves to aggravate the true causes. In contrast to what Wokeness would have us believe, the most compelling question in South Africa today is: How can we grow the economy fast enough, and develop the necessary skills base, to include millions more people in our economy through entrepreneurship and sustainable job creation?

3. Wokeness continually seeks to augment racial social engineering.

The obsession with race leads us to the false conclusion that what we need is more racial social engineering, not less. Experience worldwide, and particularly in South Africa and Zimbabwe, provides ample evidence that race based "affirmative action" does not work for the majority of disadvantaged people. In Southern Africa, it has led to cadre deployment, the spectacular enrichment of a small and connected elite, endemic corruption and a full-blown criminal State that directly exacerbates the causes of poverty.

It is a telling statistic that over the last decade of intensified race-based policies, South Africa has dropped from 1st position to 7th position in Africa on the United Nations Human Development Index, while our unemployment rate increased during that period from 21% to 32% (or 43% if we include people who have given up looking for work).

Having failed once, redoubling the imposition of race-based policies will merely aggravate exclusion.

Yet this is what our government is doing. Having inherited a statute book free of race-based laws from the National Party, following a decade-long process of dismantling legislated apartheid between 1981 and 1991, the ANC has proceeded to address the devastating legacy of race-based laws through re-introducing race-based laws!

Today, the sheer ubiquity of laws, policies, regulations, charters, codes and party diktats seeking to enforce racial exclusion on all spheres of South African life, echoes the situation under the National Party government at the height of its attempts to enforce apartheid. Once again, we are the most racially regulated society in the world.

Of course, South Africa's previous and present government had profoundly different *stated* objectives in seeking to justify race-based legislation.

But policies and laws cannot be judged primarily on the stated intentions of their promoters. They must be judged on their effect and impact. Despite the many rationalising euphemisms to justify apartheid (such as "separate development") the system had diabolical consequences, which is why so many people opposed it.

The ANC's racial policies have been codified in a plethora of BEE (later called BBBEE) laws and regulations, ostensibly to overcome the injustices of the past and make our economy more inclusive. The consequences have been the precise opposite. These laws have legalised corruption, created channels for looting, resulted in the collapse of state-owned enterprises, government departments and municipalities, and brought misery to millions.

Race laws have created an enormous barrier to investment and growth, almost killing our major job-creating industries, such as mining.

In 2019, the last year for which reliable statistics are available because of the disruption of the Covid-19 pandemic, there was a net outflow of direct investment from South Africa totalling about US$1,5 billion.

In 2017, the head of the EU Business Chamber in South Africa, Mr Stephane Sakoschek, said that European companies regarded BBBEE compliance as the single biggest deterrent to investment in South Africa. This was based on a survey of all of the Chamber's member companies.

This survey was repeated again in 2020, and BBBEE was listed once more, although this time it was the second biggest deterrent — behind the instability of electricity supply. Of course, the disruption of electricity supply was itself caused by the racial engineering and cadre deployment that had destroyed Eskom, once the most efficient electricity utility in the world. So, in effect, the two biggest deterrents to investment in South Africa are rooted in the government's policies of racial engineering.

And even during the Covid pandemic's state of disaster, the High Court ruled that government relief for small businesses had to take BBBEE criteria into account — even though businesses, irrespective of the colour of their owners and shareholders, overwhelmingly employ black staff. The result of this policy is to favour black people employed by other black people over black people who happen to work for white-owned businesses.[1]

As the *Times of London* put it some years back in an editorial on South Africa's obsession with racial transformation: "South Africa is the only country in the world where affirmative action is in the favour of the majority who has complete political control. The fact that the political majority requires affirmative action to protect them against a 9% minority group, is testament to a complete failure on their part to build their own wealth-making structures, such that their only solution is to take it from others."[2]

This commentary was clearly written before Wokeness banished such analysis from newspaper columns. But it remains true nevertheless.

And the fact that a minority (rather than a majority) is being marginalised through racial policies does not make it better. If anything, it makes it worse. A party with a built-in racial majority that legalises corruption in the interest of its ruling class under a false veneer of restorative justice will never abandon those policies.

It will continue to find new justifications until there is nothing left to steal.

4. Wokeness perpetuates and exacerbates poverty.

Opposition to race-based laws is not about protecting the vested interests of any racially defined group. The point is to broaden the benefits of economic inclusion to millions more.

It should be perfectly obvious that, with a small and rapidly shrinking economy in relation to our growing population, simply replacing white people with black people in existing jobs will not improve the circumstances of the majority of poor people, especially if the new incumbents were selected not because of their ability to perform the functions of their jobs, but rather on the basis of their political connections (behind the fig leaf of race).

Not only will the vast majority of our population remain poor and excluded, but they will be increasingly poorly serviced by an incapacitated state, and will be less able to escape their circumstances.

While the middle classes can avoid the consequences of a failed state through purchasing private sector services in healthcare, education, transport, security, electricity generation and connectivity, the poor depend on a collapsing state that is increasingly incapable of delivering the basic services the middle class takes for granted.

The primary level of governance is the local municipality that provides basic services as a foundation for human dignity — water, sanitation, refuse removal, electricity reticulation, local roads, and transport.

Increasingly, through incapacity and corruption, municipalities are unable to perform even these basic tasks.

One of the biggest scandals during 2020 was the revelation that poor municipalities had invested hundreds of millions of Rands, under false pretences, in VBS Bank, a black-owned bank whose depositors also included many impoverished rural dwellers, especially women involved in collective saving schemes.

Much of the new investment from municipalities was then creamed off in fraudulent loan schemes to politically-connected individuals, or even as grants to fund their lavish lifestyles.

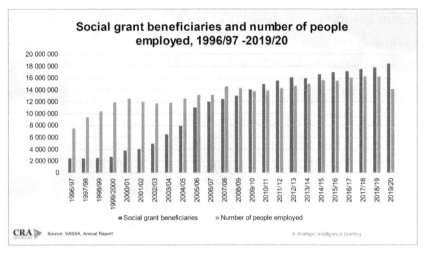

Via the Centre For Risk Analysis

When the bank went under, the life savings of thousands of poor people went down with it.

And the struggling municipalities that lost their investments are now bankrupt and even less capable of providing basic services to their impoverished communities.

Corruption partnerships between government officials and business enterprises are rife, facilitated by the requirements of "empowerment" legislation that make it easy to disguise illicit enrichment.

Delivering the keynote address at the 2019 *Financial Times* Africa Summit in London, South African President Cyril Ramaphosa highlighted this scourge when he estimated that corruption could have cost South Africa as much as R1 trillion:

"A lot of money was siphoned off the coffers of the State through corrupt means, and some of those were very sophisticated, and may I say that some of those included blue chip companies of great world reputations. It runs way beyond, in my view, more than R500 billion. Some people have even suggested that it could be a trillion Rand," said Ramaphosa.

Preferential procurement policies that set quotas for black ownership for companies to do business with the State also create a context rife for corruption.

Money that should be spent on basic service delivery is often spent enriching BBBEE "tenderpreneurs", as they are colloquially known.

In a report tabled by Johannesburg's City Power utility in the Johannesburg City Council in January 2021, listing emergency procurement for personal protective equipment during the Covid19 pandemic, an attached spreadsheet revealed that the utility had paid R3,000 for 100 ml of sanitising gel; R5,000 each for 3-ply masks; and R30,000 each for disposable surgical masks!

The DA demanded a forensic audit into what appears to be wholesale corruption in the procurement of personal protective equipment in Gauteng.

As shocking as it is, this is all small-scale corruption. Grand corruption happens in places where BBBEE requirements enable "middlemen" who add no value to a contract except meeting race quotas, to rake off millions in commissions.

To mine coal in South Africa, mining companies need to be 30% black-empowered, in line with the mining charter. However, South Africa's electricity utility Eskom (the country's biggest user of coal), arbitrarily set an informal target of 50% black-ownership for companies to supply it with coal.

To meet this target, some coal mining companies reportedly brought in "middlemen" or black trading companies, to buy the coal from the mines and then sell it to Eskom at a significant premium, passed on to the consumer through price hikes.

It is these deals that inevitably hit the poor the hardest, in the form of increased consumer costs. In the past ten years, the price of electricity has gone up 177% — 2,5 times the consumer price index of 68%.

Apart from making poor people poorer, our obsession with race diverts us from focussing on the real question that we should be obsessed about: What are the main barriers to sustainable job creation? And how do we overcome them? The national conversation should revolve around the issue of how jobs and national prosperity are created — instead of the current obsession with how *existing* jobs and resources can be taken from some and given to others.

Job creation is driven by the private sector within conditions created by a capable State. A competent, corruption-free State, that delivers basic services and ensures the rule of law, creates confidence in the future.

In that context, people who have skills, ideas, and access to capital, are prepared to take risks, start businesses, compete with others and employ job-seekers. An incapable, patronage- and race-driven State creates the opposite environment, killing confidence, growth, and jobs.

It should also be clear that racial transformation is best served by improving education and growing the number of jobs, the majority of which would go to black people, for the simple reason that whites are a shrinking minority.

However, instead of operating in a "paradigm of plenty" the ANC's policies cause jobs to shrink — inevitably leaving more and more people in hostile contestation over a diminishing jobs pool, in a "paradigm of poverty".

5. Wokeness delegitimises the goodwill and contributions of a large number of South Africans, on the basis of immutable biological characteristics.

Whether we like it or not, whites have a lot of what is necessary, such as skills and access to capital, to make South Africa successful. Much of this is attributable to the legacy of apartheid.

But we cannot change the past. We can only focus on fixing the future. The road to economic inclusion starts with ensuring that people with skills and access to capital feel confident and committed to remaining and investing in South Africa and helping to grow an inclusive economy.

The extent of the transition made by many white South Africans since the apartheid era is often underestimated. There are few examples in history where a minority group has given up all political power, through negotiations, in order to avoid escalating civil conflict.

Most white South Africans, having once voted for apartheid and segregation, embraced the new Constitution with its cornerstone value of non-racialism, while loyally continuing to pay taxes, which constitute a substantial proportion of the country's revenue base. They have done so despite skyrocketing levels of government corruption and plans to amend the Constitution to expropriate property without compensation.

Throughout the first two decades of democracy, white South Africans voted in increasing numbers in every election for an avowedly liberal party, the Democratic Alliance (DA). This represented a commitment to the non-racialism espoused by Nelson Mandela and entrenched in our founding compact, the Constitution. These voters have also accepted the need for meaningful redress to achieve economic justice, including far-reaching land reform.

This electoral shift was so meaningful precisely because it represents a conscious choice by white South Africans to reject the appeal of narrow ethnically-based parties and to support instead the non-racial liberal centre of politics.

By 2016, 93% of all white voters voted for the DA, under a black party leader, with eight out of nine black provincial leaders.

The more they are targeted as villains, and blamed for the failed policies of a corrupt government, the more racial nationalist alternatives become appealing for minorities too. This leads to a further evisceration of the moderate, non-racial centre of politics.

Scapegoating minorities has never empowered a majority, and it certainly will not do so in South Africa. On the contrary, it always ends in disaster.

6. American race "solutions" will cause much more harm than good in SA.

Importing a false diagnosis of our social pathologies from America blinds us to the fundamental difference between the impact of the proposed "cure" in our context. America's economy and institutions are independent and strong enough to withstand the ongoing assault of identity politics, as we saw in the recent stress-test imposed by Donald Trump resisting the outcome of the 2020 election.

In South Africa, nascent institutions are crumbling because we have subordinated all else to the imperative of racial transformation, which has become (and I maintain always was) a fig leaf to hide political patronage, looting, and the capture of independent state institutions to abuse power and serve individual and political objectives.

These developments predated Wokeness by almost two decades. But the international Woke Wave has had the effect of turbo charging a flagging rocket.

Because of America's resilience, it will recover from the era of Wokeness and the pendulum will find its equilibrium again. The United States may even emerge as a kinder, gentler, more empathetic society as it finds its balance.

In South Africa, when the word "Woke" goes out of fashion, its foundational ideology will remain entrenched because a rent-seeking elite that claims to represent a demographic majority, has too great a vested interest in entrenching racial preferencing.

Wokeness will not make our society more empathetic. It will make it more parasitic and kleptocratic.

Already, politics within South Africa's ruling elite is no longer engaged in a battle of ideas, but in a battle of control for the patronage machine that dispenses state tenders, deploys loyal "cadres" to positions throughout the state (and even to company boards in the private sector) and disburses funds to a range of institutions and organisations.

The ruling ANC has become an interlocking network of competing criminal syndicates, seeking to control the myriad "cash dispensers" that the state offers, rather than governing the country.

7. Wokeness is deeply sceptical of our Constitution and is destroying functional institutions. There is no road to recovery from multiple institutional collapse.

At its core, Woke ideology regards the Constitution and the institutions of liberal democracy as an alien, colonial imposition, inimical to indigenous cultures. This justifies their dismantling, in the name of "transformation."

This was the basis upon which Jesse Duarte, the Deputy Secretary General of the ANC, recently attacked the Zondo Commission of Inquiry that is investigating State Capture and Corruption. The ANC's ideology of democratic centralism, argued Duarte, "is now the subject of a commission led by a judge who, with respect, practices his craft based on the narrow parameters of existing laws. One can only hope that the Zondo Commission is not going to turn our democracy into more of a neo-liberal concoction than it already is; where we all sound the same and do nothing real to transform our society."

A clearer rejection of our Constitution and the rule of law would be hard to find.

She was subsequently forced to apologise, but her words were out there, and they are emblematic of the growing threat facing South Africa — mobilisation to dismantle the Constitution itself.

The Woke threat is not confined to the institutions of governance. Our best educational institutions, both public and private, are also under assault.

Perhaps most prominent in this regard is the University of Cape Town — Africa's premier university. Ten years ago, it would have been unthinkable to find the following motion on the agenda of the University's Convocation:

"The Alumni of UCT have witnessed with growing concern the resurgence of intolerant racial essentialism at the university. Where once this was enforced by the apartheid regime, it is now promoted by a 'woke' administration. Ever since 'Fallist' protestors were allowed to rampage across the campus without facing real sanctions — terrorising staff and students and destroying cultural objects in their attack on 'colonialism' and 'whiteness' — an atmosphere of fear has hung over the university. The Alumni also note with alarm the concerns raised by the outgoing university Ombud about bullying and the fear of retribution this provokes, undermining what should be a university 'community'. Academics have been prevented from lecturing on the campus, have had their research condemned as racially offensive without any prior due process, and many have resigned. Most tragically of all, the suicide of Professor Bongani Mayosi has been attributed in large part to the lack of adequate

support by the university and especially to aggressive condemnation on the part of Fallist students for supposedly being a race traitor. We call on the university administration to take active steps to address what is clearly becoming an increasingly racially divided and divisive culture of condemnation and bullying on campus. Urgent steps must be taken to rebuild a culture of non-racialism and to ensure that UCT becomes a place where study, research and teaching can continue unimpeded by intolerance."

This motion served at the University's convocation meeting on 18 February 2021, proposed by Martin Plaut, a UCT alumnus, former BBC World Service Africa Editor, author and Fellow of the Institute of Commonwealth Studies. It was defeated by 54 votes to 16 with 3 abstentions.

During the course of the debate, Plaut, who has an impeccable track record of fighting racism and discrimination, especially on university campuses since he was himself a student in the late 1960s and early 1970s, was predictably labelled a "neo-colonialist" and a "racist" during the meeting for supporting non-racialism!

Ultimately, it is the catastrophic combination of decline across multiple institutions that destroys a society.

One vivid recent example was highlighted by the Supreme Court of Appeal when it overturned the murder conviction of two young men, in the North West High Court, following the death of teenage boy.

It is relevant to this account to note that the two accused men were white, and the deceased boy was black.

The boy died from his injuries when he jumped off the back of a bakkie (a pickup truck) while being transported to the police station by the two men who had apprehended him for stealing sunflowers from their employer's farm.

The two men were convicted of murder and sentenced to long prison terms, on the basis of the uncorroborated and contradictory evidence of a single witness, whose credibility was torn to shreds on appeal.

The Coligny case, as it became known, after the name of the rural town where the tragedy had occurred, prompted legal analysts to note that the Appeal Court had eventually secured justice for the accused — but only by a whisker, when all the other checks and balances had already failed.

This case provided the perfect example of multiple institutional failure. Large sections of the media assumed the two white men were guilty from the start. Their reporting drove racial polarisation, justifying the Economic Freedom Fighters' (EFF) incitement of the local community to vandalise and loot the town's business district.

The police and the National Prosecuting Authority concluded that there was a case to answer, despite the lack of evidence. The High Court Judge, unable to swim against the powerful woke current, found the accused guilty.

If it were not for the famed "backbone" of the Supreme Court of Appeal, two people would have been sentenced to decades in jail on the basis of a single witness who was found to have been untruthful and self-contradictory in court.

The failing state is profoundly exacerbated by the woke *Zeitgeist* in which, irrespective of the facts, officials default to condemning whiteness in racially-charged situations. This increasingly results in a collective collapse of courage to do what is right on matters involving race. This oppressive context inevitably results in minorities feeling disempowered and unprotected by state institutions.

This factor, among many others, is profoundly corrosive and cannot be countered in the long run, destroying the fabric of society in the same way multiple organ failure kills a human body.

It is telling that Judge Ronnie Hendricks, who presided over the travesty of the Coligny High Court trial, was promoted to Deputy Judge President of the North West Province shortly after his verdict (which was ultimately overturned on appeal). No doubt, it won't be long before he seeks promotion to the Appeal Court on the basis of his woke record.

When he interviews for promotion, the ANC majority on the Judicial Service Commission is sure to be impressed by his credentials and track record on matters of race.

But perhaps the greatest tragedy is the extent to which South Africa's apex institution, the Constitutional Court, seems to be buying into the ANC's con trick of "racial transformation *uber alles*" even when this undermines key constitutional rights.

A clear example of this is the Constitutional Court's ruling that erodes the right under Section 29 of the Constitution to education in the language of choice in public education institutions, where this is reasonably practicable.

As part of the woke reign of terror unleashed across university campuses by the Fallist movement in 2016, a group of students, disguising their intent behind the benign name "Open Stellenbosch", launched an attack on Section 29 of the Constitution at

Stellenbosch University. Through an intimidation campaign of violence and vandalism, this group pushed for the abolition of Afrikaans at the university, even though it is the majority language of the Western Cape and is spoken as a primary language by millions of disadvantaged South Africans who are not white.

What made this campaign even more inexplicable was the fact that English enjoyed equal status with Afrikaans on the campus, meaning that no one was excluded from any field of study on the basis of their inability to speak Afrikaans.

However, claiming that they experienced Afrikaans as "violence" because it was associated with "whiteness" — even though the majority of Afrikaans speakers are not white — the Fallists demanded the abolition of Afrikaans as a medium of instruction.

The university authorities capitulated immediately, presumably terrified of being labelled racist. They made no attempt to defend the Section 29 rights of the thousands of Afrikaans students at the university nor the millions of Afrikaans speakers in the Western and Northern Cape, where Afrikaans speakers constitute a demographic majority.

Instead, the university's management hastily adopted a new language policy in 2016, which made English the only primary language of instruction at the university and relegated Afrikaans to a meaningless ceremonial role.

An interest group mobilising for language rights called "Gelyke Kanse" (Equal Opportunities) approached the Constitutional Court on the basis that the university had violated the constitutional right of thousands of students currently studying — and hundreds of thousands of potential future students — to receive education in their mother tongue, as has been the case at Stellenbosch for nearly 100 years.

In a blow to constitutionalism, the Constitutional Court unanimously ruled that the 2016 language policy making English the only language of tuition was permissible.

Mere weeks after writing the judgement that abolished Afrikaans tuition at Stellenbosch, Justice Edwin Cameron, who authored the Constitutional Court Judgment, was selected as the university's new chancellor.

It was a stunning victory for the woke ideology of Fallism. Through some violence and vandalism on the campus, the Fallists seemed to have been able to amend the South African Constitution by securing the scrapping of Section 29 rights to mother tongue education.

It was only through sustained counter-mobilisation that the university was pushed to review its language policy in order to reinstate the constitutional rights of Afrikaans-speaking students. It is a pity they could not rely on the Constitutional Court to protect their rights against the onslaught of Wokeness.If the precedent set in the Stellenbosch case is allowed to stand – namely that a constitutional right can be effectively nullified in this way – the "decolonisation" movement on university campuses is likely to escalate, diverting attention from the real challenges facing education.

8. Wokeness prevents us from speaking honestly about problems and solutions.

Wokeness stigmatises offensive speech — unless it is directed against biologically-defined villains, in which case any form of insult is permissible. The prohibition of anything that might be considered offensive to other groups in society prevents us from having essential conversations about how we deal with the root causes of our problems.

In the Woke hierarchy of victimhood, those endowed with a higher victimhood point score may silence speech they consider offensive by those with a lower score.

This empowers the most performatively offended people in society to set the limits on what other people may say, write, or discuss. If a topic is offensive to anyone, it is off limits for everyone. This kills free speech, the very foundational value of liberal democracy, without which social progress is impossible.

One example of a topic that is off-limits is the role that culture plays in individual and social development. This subject is totally taboo — a career extinction event to those who dare raise it.

"Woke ideology," wrote David Bern, a noted non-woke author, "has achieved a near total victory in crowding out cultural explanations for disparity in the world...The Woke have successfully branded cultural explanations as racist.[3]

If whiteness and white supremacy are truly the all-powerful force that woke ideologues make them out to be, why do so many other ethnic populations substantially out-perform whites?" asks Bern.

That question applies to South Africa as well, exemplified by South African Indians, who have used freedom, since our first democratic election in 1994, to massively advance their individual and collective circumstances. According to a study by Standard Bank published in 2016, South African Indians improved their average per capita income by 468% between 1996 and 2014.

This cannot only be due to affirmative action. There must be cultural factors at work here, such as family cohesion, prioritising education, and enterprise-orientation, but Wokeness prohibits us from even raising this possibility.

Thus, the popular explanation for the relatively rapid social and economic progress of the Indian community is rationalised by the fact that "they were not as disadvantaged as black people were under apartheid". This is a debatable premise, but a convenient way of avoiding the complex debate around culture.

We also need to address other unaskable questions such as: Why is the work ethic of so many teachers in our most disadvantaged schools so low? Why, despite our much-vaunted value of Ubuntu, do so many men abandon their children? Why is it so difficult to effect behavioural change that has profoundly negative social consequences — such as inter-generational unprotected sex with multiple partners that leaves growing numbers of young girls HIV positive and pregnant?

While all this remains unspoken, it is entirely acceptable in the new climate to rage against "cultural whiteness".

Sensitivity training in major corporates (which is often a quaint label to disguise reverse racism) requires employees to accept, unquestioningly, racist tropes about white people and their supposed culture.

In major American firms, courses are sometimes mandatory to assist employees to "try to be less white", associating a range of negative stereotypes with "whiteness", such as arrogance, defensiveness, apathy, and oppressiveness. This kind of racism is being swallowed wholesale, and the outcome in South Africa is hardly likely to be the inter-racial social cohesion we need.

For as long as Wokeness forbids us from addressing some cultural questions, while accepting others as race-determined, for so long will cultural factors put a brake on progress.

And for as long as whites and "whiteness" remain convenient scapegoats for negative social and economic outcomes, for so long will we fail to address the root causes of our problems.

9. Wokeness makes it much, much harder to find a democratic way out of this dead end through the ballot box.

The Democratic Alliance's challenge has always been to build a new majority in South Africa, based on *values*, not race, in order to challenge the ANC for power in elections.

In the process, during my term as leader, I often described DA-supporting South Africans, whatever their race, as blue people exemplifying "blue values" — a commitment to constitutionalism, the rule of law, non-racialism, and a social market economy.

These values are the direct antithesis of the ANC's kleptocratic ideology of racial nationalism and state control of the economy. Race mobilisation has always been a formidable — but not totally insurmountable — obstacle to building a new "blue" majority. However, Wokeness makes it much, much harder to do this because it regards "race essentialism" (prioritising race over everything else) as "progressive".

And, in the context of the primeval power of race mobilisation, minorities are, in the main, unable to stop this downward slide by voting the ANC out. The tragedy of the Woke *Zeitgeist* is that it has justified and fortified the race essentialism that will lead to South Africa's demise.

10. Wokeness destroys our capacity to build a South African Nation.

Arguably, South Africa's foundational challenge is building a common sense of nationhood. This will be achieved when all citizens regard themselves — and each other — as South Africans first, before defining themselves, or another person, on the basis of their race, gender, sexual orientation, or other personal and immutable characteristics.

Nelson Mandela made nation-building and reconciliation his overriding priority, establishing a sense of belonging among all South Africans and a widespread consensus that the country was heading in the right direction, promising a better future for all.

Wokeness fails to recognise the importance of a sense of nationhood, as it pushes the country back into racial enclaves.

With devastating centrifugal force, it is driving people apart on the basis of their biology and shattering social cohesion in a manner increasingly reminiscent of apartheid.

There is one fundamental difference between American and South African Wokeness though:

In America, Wokeness claims to promote the rights of minorities.

In South Africa, Wokeness openly targets minorities, especially if they are white.

That is a profound difference. And for as long as high-achieving minorities are type-cast as permanent villains on the basis of race, for so long will South Africa's major export be its capital and skills — which no emerging country can afford to lose.

Least of all South Africa, which depends on a tiny proportion of the population to disproportionately fund the fiscus. According to financial journalist Bruce Whitfield (*Financial Mail* 27 February 2020), out of 14-million people registered as taxpayers in South Africa, only 4% of them (574 000 people) pay over 50% of personal taxes, the largest revenue source for government, which in 2019 totalled R548.6bn. An even smaller sub-group - 125 000 taxpayers - contributed R150bn of this total.

This brings home, in a very literal sense, how easy it is for a country like South Africa to go broke, which we effectively are already.

So, what is to be done?

Should liberals meekly sit back and accept their fate, trapped between the growing populist Right and Wokeness? Should we just go down quietly?

For me the answer is an emphatic No! Although there is much less room for optimism today than there was at the dawn of our democracy, we cannot give up on the quest for a non-racial democracy, governed by the rule of just law, without a fight.

There is too much at stake to walk away now. If South Africa's democratic project fails, the consequences are grave, not only for all who live in the country, but for the continent too. And it augurs very poorly for other divided societies seeking to overcome conflict between competing ethnic and racial groups, while striving to build inclusive, economically-prosperous democracies.

The last chapter sets out some things we can do to regain the promise of freedom.

What South Africans Can Do to Resist Wokeness

IN HIS BOOK *The Case for Democracy*, published in 2004, Natan Sharansky set down his famous explanation of what it means to live in a free society:

"If a person cannot walk into the middle of the town square and express his or her views without fear of arrest, imprisonment, or physical harm, then that person is living in a fear society, not a free society. We cannot rest until every person living in a 'fear society' has finally won their freedom."

Sharansky, who had spent nine years (1977-1986) in a Soviet prison for "high treason", and who was eventually released as part of a prisoner swap with the West, knew all about living in a fear society.

Settling in Israel on his release, he continued his activism for freedom (and against anti-Semitism).

The Case for Democracy, a foreign policy manifesto to advance freedom in the world, which includes his famous definition of freedom, was clearly writing in a pre-digital age.

How has social media changed our understanding of what it is to live in a fear society, where people shrink away from expressing their opinions for fear of online persecution?

"Wrongspeak" may not be punished directly by physical harm, but through psychological harassment and public "cancelling" reminiscent of the tactics of repressive totalitarian regimes.

A necessary condition for freedom, as understood by Sharansky, is an environment where people engage in debate and argument because they are interested in the truth, and believe that the dialectic method helps get them closer to it. In this environment, reason and evidence determine the value of an argument.

Neither he, nor anyone else, could have foreseen that free societies, using the technology intended to broaden access to public debate, would in fact divide people into thought-silos, kept apart by algorithms that feed them a diet of their own biases, while encouraging them to abandon all norms of rational and civil discourse, behind a cloak of anonymity.

This tendency was significantly intensified because it coincided with the dramatic rise of identity politics (otherwise known as Wokeness), which as a quasi-religious ideology, requires unwavering faith in, and adherence to, its doctrines.

To challenge and question them is heresy, deserving of the strongest censure — being cast out of society through an online *fatwa,* or digital witch-burning.

This represents a fundamental paradigm shift from the era of rational discourse, and the secular search for truth. Subjective feelings trump scientifically verifiable facts, which are often dismissed for negating the ultimate truth of "lived experience".

The stock in trade of online conversations are the extremes of shaming or virtue-signalling. The rational centre is eviscerated through performative moral grandstanding.

The most important thing we can do to stop this rising fundamentalist tide is to have the courage to speak out against it.

It takes enormous courage and principled determination to stand up against the encroachment of the "fear society". Having lived through the apartheid era, as an outspoken critic, I find it harder to question the tenets of Wokeness today than it was to speak out against racist policies and prejudices 40 years ago.

That may not be true for everyone, but it is my personal, lived experience.

In this kind of context, it is always easier to keep quiet, or join the charade — but we betray our democracy, and the right to free speech that underpins it, if we do.

So, below, I give guidelines for conversations on "taboo" subjects which Wokeness has decreed to be off-limits to any challenge. These are followed by examples of such conversations.

The key tips for engaging Wokes on sensitive topics are:

1. Before you begin, marshal your facts. The previous
   chapter sought to provide a factual basis to challenge the
   politics of racial identity (the most common form of

applied Wokeness in South Africa.) It is important to have facts at your fingertips because it is difficult to remain focused and rational when you are facing an avalanche of emotion expressed in language you may be unfamiliar with.

2. Unless you are extremely brave, and are prepared to face being "cancelled", preferably avoid having these conversations on Twitter. It is a hostile, hot mess of moral indignation looking for a place to settle. If your tweet crosses a woke firing line, prepare to be met by a volley of artillery fire until you are permanently silenced and possibly fired from your job. However, it is useful to venture into less loathsome spaces, such as Facebook, if you have enough guts and determination.

3. While engaging with someone who inhabits another "thought- silo", either personally or online, listen, but don't allow yourself to be trampled on.

4. When these conversations happen in groups, you may find yourself alone in holding a different opinion. Don't be cowed into silence. State your case calmly and rationally.

5. See if it is possible to find common ground. If it proves impossible, stand your ground, but don't hesitate to acknowledge a good point made by your adversary.

6. Be aware that a woke opponent seeks to silence you by making you feel guilty, even if you can back up your argument with evidence. Try to remain impervious to the emotionally charged discourse even if it denigrates, belittles, invalidates, and eventually cancels you from the conversation, while failing to deal with the merits of your argument.

7. It is hard to remain calm in such situations, but it helps to be aware that the core tactic of Wokeness is to mobilise emotional rage, create a public spectacle and force agreement through psychological manipulation and character assassination. It certainly works with a lot of people who will be silenced, even if they agree with you.

8. Don't be afraid to stand alone. You are *not* on the wrong side of history. Merely standing up for free speech puts you on the right side of history.

9. Take note of logical fallacies and factual errors in the argument. Rationally point them out when you get your chance to speak. If you do not get a chance to speak against the torrent of words, calmly insist on having an opportunity.

10. Distinguish between facts and "lived experience". Lived experience can be helpful in informing arguments, but is not a substitute for facts or a basis for invalidating alternative opinions.

11. Don't take it personally, or become personal, even if they do.

12. Do not think you can win an argument with a Social Justice Warrior (SJW). This is impossible. But don't let that prevent you from stating your case unless the conversation is totally inappropriate to the situation (Wokes tend not to apply that level of discretion).

I provide some sample conversations below. Although the conversations are fictional, they are based on real life examples.

One of the participants in each of the discussions below is an SJW. I use the description in the sense defined by the urban dictionary as an individual who repeatedly and vehemently engages in arguments on social justice issues, often (but not exclusively) on the internet, usually in a shallow way, for the purpose of enhancing their own personal reputation.

In the previous chapter, I focused particularly on arguments to counter SJWs on the subject of race. So, here I will start with another topic – a sample conversation about the current cause célèbre of Wokeness: Transgender rights.

The background is a true story: A friend of mine, a construction project manager by profession, told me he had recently overseen the building of a new high school, where, in line with the latest progressive specifications, the toilets were unisex.

At the school's open day, when prospective students and their families were invited to come and look around, many parents (especially of girls) were horrified. They insisted that, if their children were enrolled at the school, the girls' bathrooms would have to be separated from the boys'.

After a period of intense debate, single sex toilets were re-introduced to the school, and peace was restored.

Based on this real-life experience, I have recreated the following fictional discussion between a mother of a girl at the school and an SJW championing "trans rights".

Mother: I am uncomfortable with the idea of unisex toilets, to the point that I will not enrol my daughter at this school unless this is changed.

SJW: You are clearly a bigoted transphobe.

Mother: A what?

SJW: A transphobe. You are denying the right of transsexual teenage girls to use bathrooms in a space where they can feel comfortable in, and be themselves. When there are gendered bathrooms, every time a trans girl wants to go to the bathroom she has to violate her identity.

Mother: I do not want to violate anyone's identity. But I really think there are some spaces where girls need to feel safe, and school toilets are among them. What's more, girls going through puberty and dealing with the on-set of their menstrual cycle have different ablution requirements from boys. They are entitled to an added level of privacy at this sensitive time.

SJW: Are you saying that young people who identify as female, but who do not menstruate, are not proper girls? That is insulting and marginalises all trans women. This is the violence of their daily lived experience. What's more, your child is being raised in a transphobic home, and learning these same bigoted opinions.

Mother: Please do not get personal. I respect your argument but I do not agree with it. Girls and boys going through puberty require separate toilets. My own experience of growing up, and the long struggle by feminists for safe spaces, inform my belief that there is too much risk for girls in unisex toilets. I agree that this does create a dilemma for trans girls. But then we must look for a reasonable way of addressing that dilemma without denying the rights of girls, who identify as girls on the basis of their physiology, to use separate bathrooms.

SJW: There is no point in talking to a fascist like you.

Mother: Perhaps you should focus on the merit of my argument and stop your personal insults. We have a competing set of rights here, and that makes the issue complex. It is not a solution to negate the rights of some in order to advance the rights of others, however legitimate. I want trans girls to be free to be themselves, but I would like you to recognise the risk to women of abandoning some spaces reserved for their exclusive use. We must talk this through until we find a way of dealing with the matter that respects everyone's rights.

SJW: You have revealed yourself as a TERF.

Mother: What is a TERF?

SJW: Go and Google it. I do not waste my breath on them...

In case you are unfamiliar with the acronym, a TERF is a trans-exclusionary radical feminist, (which the woman in this account certainly is not). But TERF is a pejorative label used against all those who believe that the enforced abandoning of the physiological definition of womanhood is a setback for feminist struggles in many fields, from sport, to rape shelters, prisons, girls-only schools, and changing rooms.

In other words, they believe it is wrong that any man who claims to identify as a woman, can be allowed to inhabit, or compete in fields or institutions previously reserved for women, physiologically defined. They regard this as a setback for women's rights.

My second example deals with the well known American slogan that grew out of the #MeToo movement: "Believe Women". It requires the unquestioning acceptance of allegations made by women of sexual harassment against men.

While this default may often be valid, there is enormous danger in believing it always is. Each case has to be treated on its own merits.

The background: Late in 2020, I wrote an article analysing the profound injustice committed by the media against a male leader in the Democratic Alliance (DA) accused of sexual harassment by a woman, whose account could be easily dismantled, and whose motive was clearly apparent.

I received a lot of private and positive feedback on the article, but across the board, supporters kept their heads below the parapet. One of them ended his congratulatory note with the following comment: "Of course I could never express my appreciation of your article in a public forum and therein lies the problem".

Indeed, it does.

So, I have created a fictional conversation on this incident between an SJW and myself. I have changed the names of the protagonists. Otherwise the details are true:

SJW: The fact that the DA fired Nomsa immediately after she made allegations of sexual harassment against Sam shows what a sexist organisation the DA is. It will always protect its male leaders irrespective of what they do to women.

Me: I'm afraid you have your facts wrong, but I can understand why. The media have reported it that way, although it isn't the truth.

SJW: Stop rationalising and justifying the DA's sexism.

Me: I think this conversation would benefit from some background information. Nomsa had her DA membership terminated for leaking confidential caucus strategy to the Economic Freedom Fighters. Sam had given evidence against her. After an exhaustive three-year internal disciplinary process, including appeals, the evidence against her was overwhelming and incontrovertible.

When she knew she had lost the case, and her days as a party member were numbered, she alleged Sam had sexually harassed her in an incident that allegedly took place six years ago. The timing of her allegation is rather strange, and Sam emphatically denies it.

SJW: How dare you question the timing! Women who feel violated have a right to raise this at any time, when they feel it is appropriate to do so. It may have been difficult six years ago to raise the issue because Sam was her senior in the organisation. But if she says it now, why are you questioning her?

Me: I am questioning her motives for raising this at a point when she has run out of options to save her DA membership, and her lucrative position as a public representative.

During the six years since this harassment incident is alleged to have happened, she enjoyed a cordial professional relationship with Sam, as evidenced by the fact that she invited him to give the main speech at her birthday celebration, and praised him in multiple social media posts. It seems very strange to suddenly come up with an allegation that you were traumatised by an incident of sexual harassment, just as you are about to be fired for serious misconduct.

SJW: This is how the sexual abuse of women is perpetuated. They aren't believed. They are questioned. They are violated a second time when they dare to speak out.

Me: That is certainly the case in some instances, but not in this one. According to Nomsa's own version (that Sam denies), he put his hand on her knee and said "I want you" — and the matter ended there. On her own account, there was no further advance from his side. Let's for the sake of argument assume that events happened as she says they did. Regarding that as a violation that still traumatises you six years later is perhaps a bit of a stretch.

SJW: How dare you question the lived experience of a woman in a subordinate position. If she felt violated, she was violated.

Me: Maybe she isn't the innocent party in this case. Maybe the violence of intentional reputation destruction makes Sam the victim of a woman with a motive. The hashtag #BelieveWomen cannot be allowed to eradicate the rule of law. We all believe in the principle "Innocent until proven guilty". But #BelieveWomen means innocent in perpetuity because of your chromosome configuration. That can't be right.

SJW: I cannot speak to a sexist bigot like you.

―――

My third example is based on something that most South Africans will be familiar with.

It is an imaginary conversation between an SJW and a rugby fan about the dramatic studio walk-out by former rugby commentator, Ashwin Willemse, during a live television broadcast of the Super-Sport pay channel.

A black former Springbok, Willemse lashed out at his fellow white commentators, Naas Botha and Nick Mallett, in protest against what he described as racist and patronising behaviour on their part.

The drama played out following a match between the Lions and the Brumbies in 2018, stunning viewers.

In mid-broadcast, Ashwin walked over to where Naas and Nick were sitting and told them he "can't work with people who under-mine other people" and that he was "glad this is happening on live TV so that people can see".

He said he rejected being "patronised by two individuals who played in an apartheid/segregated era" and referenced the deroga-tory label "quota players", to describe players suspected of having been selected to fill race quotas.

The incident set social media alight. Unsurprisingly, Twitter instantly convicted Nick Mallet and Naas Botha of racism. Ex-players, the sports minister, political leaders, journalists, and the usual swarm of trolls came out in full support of Ashwin's actions and commended him for taking a stand against racism through his prime-time protest.

Nick and Naas were subjected to the full shaming ritual cycle in the course of three hours.

SuperSport suspended all three, and instituted its own investiga-tion, headed by a senior advocate, Mr Vincent Maleka SC, assisted by the then Vice-Chancellor of the University of the Witwater-srand, Professor Adam Habib, who is considered an expert in various overt and covert forms of racism.

Ashwin Willemse refused to give evidence to the investigation, preferring to take his case directly to Buang Jones, the controversial Acting Provincial Manager of the South African Human Rights Commission (SAHRC) based in another province, who has been involved in a different public spat involving a rugby player, where he pronounced on "white guilt" before being in possession of the facts. Buang Jones seized the Willemse case with alacrity, calling for public submissions to support his claim of racism at *SuperSport*.

The Maleka investigation concluded that the incident involving Willemse, Mallett, and Botha involved neither "naked racism" nor "subtle racism" and that a misunderstanding had given rise to the contretemps.

To date (three years after the incident), the SAHRC's investigation under Buang Jones has not yet issued any report on the matter. I followed up to find out why and was told: "The matter was never completed. We closed the file due to the unavailability of Mr Willemse."

He has made no use of any opportunity to state his case, even when he was granted his requested opportunity from the institution of his choice.

When Willemse's contract with *SuperSport* ended, it was not renewed. Both Mallett and Botha are now back on air.

SJW: It is an absolute outrage that *SuperSport* was allowed to get away with its institutional racism against black rugby commentators, and that Nick Mallett and Naas Botha are back on air, as if nothing had happened.

Rugby fan: What evidence do you have of institutional racism against black rugby commentators at *SuperSport*? There are several excellent black commentators on air whose commentary is respected by all rugby fans. Not because they are black, but because they have a deep knowledge of the game.

SJW: Those guys are just too frightened of losing their jobs to speak out. At least Ashwin Willemse had the courage to take a stand, and did so publicly. He paid a high price by not having his contract renewed, but he made the sacrifice to expose institutional racism.

Rugby Fan: I am sure that there are individual incidents of racism in rugby as there are everywhere else. But to draw the conclusion that racism is institutionalised either in rugby or at *SuperSport* is a stretch. Supersport instituted an investigation into the facts that led to Willemse's walk-out. The investigation was led by a prominent black advocate, who found that there was neither overt or subtle racism involved.

SJW: They are all sell-outs. Who are they to deny Ashwin's lived experience, and his courage to speak out?

Rugby Fan: Have you ever considered that there may have been other factors involved? The investigation highlighted a potential misunderstanding involving speaking turns. Because Ashwin did not have a turn after the previous game between the Sharks and the Chiefs, both Mallett and Botha stood back to enable him to comment first on the Lions/Brumbies game. He interpreted that as patronising. Surely this is something that can be discussed and resolved by adults over a beer, rather than end up as a public fracas, with pejorative labels being pinned to people?

SJW: This is typical of Whiteness. Always looking for superficial solutions that do not resolve the underlying problems of institutional racism. Can't you understand that Ashwin would have experienced their actions as the typical patronising white attitude? As if he couldn't come into the conversation when he chose to do so! These are the sorts of micro-aggressions black people experience every day.

Rugby Fan: Well, if Naas and Nick had not allowed him the first speaking turn, that would have been interpreted as racist as well. You just can't win when whatever you do is interpreted as racist.

SJW: There you go again, refusing to recognise the systemic racism manifesting itself in the situation.

Rugby Fan: I think we'll have to agree to disagree.

SJW: Get lost, you Nazi!

———

Holding the line at the level of personal interaction is the crucial first line of defence in a free society.

Simply having the courage to speak out (when everyone else is cowed into silent conformity) is the foundation for all the other steps necessary to prevent Wokeness from turning South Africa into a fear society.

This is far more difficult to do than most people think. A few widely-publicised "cancellings" or "shamings" are all it takes to enforce Woke narratives and silence opposition, or drive it underground.

That is why a new initiative, called Counterweight, is so welcome.

Founded by the British liberal academic and editor, Helen Pluck-rose, Counterweight is a "non-partisan, grassroots movement, advocating for liberal concepts of social justice to help individuals resist the imposition of Critical Social Justice on their day-to-day lives", according to Pluckrose's Wikipedia entry.

Counterweight draws together academics, students, psychologists, parents, and a range of professionals from different fields into a mutual support network to stand against "mob rule", in support of individual freedom. It is far easier to speak up if you know you are not alone, and can seek the help you need.

This is precisely what we need in South Africa, (and I would put up my hand to lead its local branch if I did not already have a more than full-time job). In the meantime, I have joined Counter-weight online. If enough South Africans take this step, we can form a local support network for people who become the targets of Wokery's arbitrary cruelties.

Despite the liberal focus on the primacy of the individual, group solidarity is indispensable in standing up for the values that free societies hold dear, especially in the face of authoritarian ideologies. Individuals alone cannot possibly stand firm against the Woke tide. Never has it been more crucial for us to work together, at every level, to defend and promote values that are essential for South Africa to succeed.

Unlike established democracies, the consequences of Wokeness in South Africa has given rise to a range of existential fears, the most significant of which is the threat of living under a rapidly failing state.

Successful democracies, according to author and political-economist, Francis Fukuyama, are built on three pillars: the rule of law, a capable state, and a societal culture of accountability.

South Africa is in the intensive care unit on all three counts.

The failing state affects everyone's quality of life. Dirty potholed streets, electricity blackouts, sewage seepages, water outages, failing hospitals and schools, a dysfunctional criminal justice system, and bankrupt municipalities unable to perform the most rudimentary functions, are features of daily life for many (but not all) South Africans.

As usual, South Africa's customary resilience has been apparent in the face of this growing crisis.

There have been four major responses:

1. The development by the private sector of a "parallel state" providing world-class services for the middle class, at a price.
2. The Afrikaner community working to secure group-based immunity from state failure, including protection of their language and cultural rights, irrespective of class status.
3. A growing secessionist movement in areas of the country where minorities, working together, can constitute an electoral majority.
4. The re-doubling of efforts to enable and encourage South Africans to escape the shackles of "demographic democracy", so that a new majority can emerge, comprising people of all races, voting for ideas and policies rather than reverting to racial identity.

These options are not mutually exclusive. For example, most people of any demographic, who can afford to buy private services, tend to do so in preference to relying on a failing state.

They can buy their services while simultaneously supporting any of the other responses to state failure I have listed.

Below, I deal with each category of response individually.

The Private Sector

South Africa's highly-capacitated private sector has effectively built a parallel state, enabling the middle class to pay for a wide variety of services, such as education, healthcare, security, transport, electricity, connectivity, amongst others.

In some towns, a strongly dominant industry will sometimes take over the service delivery role of the municipality to prevent complete collapse. This is the case in some platinum mining centres of the North West Province, where the mines fund and perform many local government services, free of charge, to ensure the provision of clean water, electricity, and refuse removal, amongst other services.

While this is a humane and necessary intervention, it shields the majority of voters from the practical consequences of their electoral choices.

Private individuals have also stepped into the breach, shielding themselves and their families from regular electricity blackouts by "going off the grid" through generating their own solar power. This is increasingly supplemented by "wheeling" agreements, which enables businesses and individuals to sell excess electricity to others.

To secure their own water supply, those who can afford it often sink boreholes, harvest and store rain water, clean the streets outside their homes, maintain their sidewalks, and sometimes even the public parks and neighbourhood trees.

But this has not solved the crisis of state failure for the poor — who ironically continue overwhelmingly to vote for the government that continues to fail them, a testament to the power of identity politics.

Nor has private sector intervention solved the crisis of state failure for functions that only the state can provide – most particularly the gradual crumbling of the criminal justice pipeline. The key role of the state is to keep citizens safe through upholding the constitution and the law. The private sector alone cannot compensate for corrupt police, an inert prosecutorial system, under-resourced forensic laboratories, and a judiciary increasingly shot through with the consequences of cadre deployment by an ANC-dominated Judicial Service Commission.

This is where the rubber of state failure hits the road of the rule-of-law. The result is an unending series of legal pile-ups with profound consequences, until the central pillar of democracy, our constitution, collapses.

In short, while the private sector continues to make life bearable for many citizens, it cannot protect South Africa entirely from all the consequences of the failing state.

Afrikaner Solidarity

This phenomenon warrants some attention because it constitutes the largest mobilisation of civil society in Africa aimed at warding off the impact of state failure and, in particular, defending the rights and interests of a minority group with a shared history, language and culture.

Afrikaners in South Africa are descended from 17th century Dutch, French, and German settlers who developed their own language and culture in the process of establishing themselves on the southern tip of Africa. The word "Afrikaner" means "African" in Dutch.

Unlike English speakers, Afrikaners do not have a worldwide cultural and linguistic community to fall back on. As the "white tribe of Africa", they have faced an existential crisis for centuries.

Living in a "fear society" is therefore not a new experience for them. It has resulted in a significant level of self-reliance and rugged individualism, combined with a very high degree of ethnic social cohesion.

Afrikaners do not regard themselves as colonisers in South Africa, in the same way that people of European descent do not regard themselves as colonisers in the United States. Like Americans, they point to their history of resisting British colonialism to under-score their right to be regarded as indigenous South African citizens.

When the Dutch established their refreshment station at the Cape of Good Hope in 1652 (followed by a gradually growing settle-ment), the great migration of the Bantu African people was well underway down the eastern coast of South Africa. The original inhabitants of South Africa, the Khoi and the San, suffered a near genocide through the pincer movement by white settlers from the South West and black migrants from the North East. The remnants of these persecuted "first peoples" retreated into the inhospitable desert terrain of the country's western interior to escape total decimation.

Afrikaners trekked away from the Cape Peninsula, first to escape the dictates of the Dutch East India Company and later British colonialism. In the 19th century, Afrikaners established two independent Boer Republics, that both gained international recognition (including by Britain): the Orange Free State in the centre of the country and the South African Republic (ZAR) further north.

The discovery of diamonds around Kimberley (in the then Free State) around 1867, attracted the attention of the British, who promptly annexed the area around Kimberley in 1873, under the ruse of protecting the Griqua people. In truth, most of the Griqua were subsequently forced to sell their farms to whites.

The real purpose of the annexation was to gain control over the diamond fields.

The British attempt to annex the ZAR in the late 1870s was met with fierce resistance, culminating in a victory for the Boers in the First Boer War, and a peace agreement formalised through the London Convention.

However, the discovery of gold on the Witwatersrand (in the ZAR) in 1886, resulted in the influx of thousands of British citizens, who paid taxes but had no civic representation. The resulting tensions led to the Second Anglo Boer War, which ended with the defeat of the Boers.

The former ZAR became Britain's "Transvaal Colony".

An estimated 13% of the Afrikaner population of the two former Republics was killed in this war, mainly in British concentration camps or in combat. This calculation is based on the 36,400 deaths out of a Boer population in the two Republics of an estimated 273,000 in 1898.

The result was the devastating impoverishment of the Afrikaners, following the British scorched earth policy that destroyed farms, and forced Afrikaners into the cities, where they performed unskilled labour, often in the mines working for British companies.

These events, as well as the British attempts to eradicate Afrikaans as a language of instruction in schools, kindled a potent nationalism in the Afrikaners, rooted in identity politics, and a vehement rejection of British imperialism.

The two former Boer Republics, now under British control, were incorporated into the Union of South Africa in 1910, which excluded black South Africans from the franchise. This, in turn, fuelled the growth of African nationalism and contributed to the growing racial divide in the country.

Over the space of almost half a century, the mobilisation of Afrikaner nationalism led to victory at the whites-only ballot box in 1948, after which Afrikaners sought to resolve their existential insecurity permanently through partition — the Balkanization of South Africa — into separate ethnic "states" where the different ethnic groups were supposed to govern themselves.

Known as "apartheid", this policy resulted in profound injustice and oppression, which has been exhaustively documented. Over time, a worldwide "anti-apartheid" movement was mobilised, including sanctions. Eventually, as resistance to apartheid escalated inside the country, its sustained imposition became untenable, and the National Party began dismantling the legislative underpinnings of the policy between 1981 and 1991, leading to constitutional negotiations for the enfranchisement of all South Africans.

The outcome — a negotiated progressive Constitution built on the principles of non-racialism and human rights — was described as a miracle.

Given South Africa's history, this unlikely outcome was indeed to be celebrated. But the need for compromise inevitably embedded serious flaws in the new Constitution. One of them was the decision to opt for a unitary state rather than a federation — which would have been far better suited to South Africa's complex historical and demographic circumstances.

South Africa's first national democratic elections were held between 26-29 April 1994, and most citizens breathed a collective sigh of relief as the country turned a crucial corner. But the daunting task of reconciliation and restitution lay ahead.

Non-racialism as the foundation of "a better life for all" was Nelson Mandela's promise, echoing his famous Speech from the Dock in his Treason Trial in which he had sought to assuaged fears of racial domination when he said:

"It is not true that the enfranchisement of all will result in racial domination.

Political division, based on colour, is entirely artificial and, when it disappears, so will the domination of one colour group by another. The ANC has spent half a century fighting against racialism. When it triumphs it will not change that policy."

The vast majority of South Africans, from all backgrounds, accepted that promise (albeit it three decades later) and committed to work within the parameters of a non-racial Constitution, promising equal rights to all, and redress for the injustices of the past.

It is easy to overlook the enormous transition made by Afrikaners, led by President FW de Klerk, in this process. The trope of a recalcitrant group of reactionary racists is entirely unwarranted. After the advent of democracy, a growing number of Afrikaners began to vote for an avowedly liberal, non-racial party, the Democratic Alliance. By 2016, well over 90% of Afrikaners voted for a party with a black leader and eight out of nine black provincial leaders, under the slogan "One Nation, One Future".

This was a profound change towards building a common nationhood.

The tragic truth is that the ANC's commitment to an inclusive, non-racial democracy, underpinned by liberal state institutions, proved to be paper-thin. It was merely a convenient stepping stone, necessitated by the international and local "balance of forces" at the time of the constitutional negotiations in the early 1990s.

The ANC was quite open, inside its own forums and in its internal documents, about moving beyond the first "bourgeois stage" of the revolution, before initiating the second stage — a step taken in 2012 — towards African nationalist socialism, also known as "democratic centralism", or the National Democratic Revolution (NDR).

This ideology exists in extreme tension with our liberal democratic Constitution, which is being eroded at every turn as the ANC capture state institutions, and use them to protect the party and its leaders from public accountability during the ensuing looting and plundering spree of state resources.

At the dawn of our democracy, a small group of Afrikaners sensed the risks ahead and decided, while hoping for the best, to prepare for the worst.

"We were derided when, during the sunshine years of the Mandela presidency, we started building an ark for the flood that we anticipated might come," wrote Flip Buys, Chairman of the Solidarity Movement, an umbrella structure which incorporates a range of Afrikaner support organisations.

They knew the odds were against South Africa becoming an inclusive non-racial democracy, despite the ANC's heady public promises. Understanding the pull of identity politics themselves, they knew that it was far more likely that South Africa would become a "demographic democracy" where elections would turn into a racial census, rather than a reflection of the informed choices of individuals assessing competing policy options.

After the ANC's 1997 Congress when it formally adopted the policy of cadre deployment to capture state institutions, state failure became a foregone conclusion, says Buys.

Because most Afrikaners have no other home but South Africa, they regarded it as incumbent upon themselves to create conducive conditions to remain in the country, and flourish, working as a community, together with other communities.

The Solidarity Movement emerged from humble beginnings in 1997/8.

It now comprises more than 500,000 families working together in 25 organisations, covering almost every aspect of social and cultural life, public safety, education and training, social services, language, cultural cohesion, and legal support. They have also identified key towns where they provide public services — for all — to compensate for a bankrupt and failing state.

In these towns, everybody benefits from the improved services, not just Afrikaners.

In a recent significant legal victory, in a class action suit brought by a group of farmers affiliated to the Solidarity Movement, the Eastern Cape High Court ordered the provincial government and local authorities to take the necessary action to maintain the rural road network within a given time, failing which the farmers could obtain three quotes to have the work done, and give the relevant authorities a deadline to accept one of them. The local and/or provincial government would then have to pay for the private delivery of the service they had failed to render.

In this, and other path-breaking judgments, courts have recognised the right of citizens to defend themselves from the consequences of a failing state — and to be compensated for the costs involved.

This trend is likely to escalate as citizens realise they are on their own, and demand some value for the taxes they pay.

As it is, members of the Afrikaner Solidarity Movement already pay a double tax — to the state, as well as an additional amount to the network of organisations that provides a safety net from the consequences of a failed state.

The Afrikaner Solidarity Movement is identity politics at its most constructive and benign.

It has much in common with the worldwide Jewish solidarity movement that looks after Jewish minorities wherever they happen to be in the world, as far as health, education, and security are concerned. The idea among Afrikaners is to work to protect each other from state failure and persecution, and to be able to continue living in the country of their forefathers.

Apart from this distinctive Solidarity Movement, there are thousands of charities and non-governmental organisations in South Africa seeking, in a multiplicity of ways, to compensate for a failing state. Prominent among them are the Islamic welfare organisation, Gift of the Givers. However, it is obviously impossible for charities to replace a functional state in a population of 58 million people.

But this is no reason why culturally cohesive minorities should not seek to protect themselves from state failure, as Afrikaners are already doing with considerable success, while benefitting others in the process.

The Secessionists

There are different groups of secessionists in South Africa who are taking self-reliance to the next level. They are demanding self-governance.

The oldest such project in South Africa is Orania — the name of a place and a small political movement which turned apartheid's ideology on its head. During the 1980s, before the end of apartheid, a group of Afrikaners had reached the conclusion that the policy was untenable because it would be impossible to balkanise South Africa into separate states for each of the 11 ethnic cultural groups.

Instead, the Orania movement sought out a small enclave of its own, as the basis for independence from the rest of South Africa. They now own a tiny enclave of about nine square kilometres of semi-desert scrubland near the Orange River in the Northern Cape. Here, they are building the very small town of Orania, which they consider the nucleus of a future "homeland" for Afrikaners who wish to govern themselves, maintaining their language and culture while escaping state failure and majority domination.

The 2011 census counted 892 souls in Orania, and it would be hard to say whether their numbers have grown or shrunk since then. This community predicts that the global shift to self-determination for minorities in complex plural societies, as well as the continued collapse of the South African state, will lead to a rapid increase in the number of people seeking refuge in Orania — and bring them a step closer to making a legitimate claim for self-government as a viable community under Section 235 of the South African Constitution.

A new, different and vocal secessionist movement has sprung up in the Western Cape — the only province not governed by the ANC. Since 2009, the Western Cape has been governed by the DA, which has traditionally been supported by minority ethnic groups in South Africa — white, coloured (mixed-race), Indian, and a relatively small percentage of black South Africans.

Apart from the provincial government, most provincial towns, including the world-renowned Cape Town, are also governed by the DA either with an overall majority or in multi-party coalitions.

It is generally recognised that the Western Cape government and its towns are better governed and far more functional than those in the rest of the country.

This has helped drive the secessionist movement, agitating for the province's full independence from South Africa.

Those who wish to see the Western Cape secede are calling on the province's premier (the equivalent of a state governor in the USA) to use his powers under Section 127.2(f) of the Constitution to call a referendum on the issue.

They predict a majority of provincial voters would support their proposal.

Then they would base their claim to independence on Section 235 of the Constitution, which opens the door for "the right of self-determination of any community sharing a common cultural and language heritage with a territorial entity in the Republic" (although they might find it challenging to meet the definition of "community" contained in that clause).

However, the problem with both Sections 127 and 235 of the Constitution, is that they cannot be implemented without enabling national legislation, which does not exist. The South African government, with its ANC majority, is clearly in no particular hurry to fill this legislative void.

In the absence of such legislation, secession cannot happen by peaceful means.

While there are some notable examples of secession worldwide, such as the former Soviet Republics exiting the Soviet Union, or Ireland leaving the United Kingdom, there are far more examples of failed secessions, mired in conflicts that last decades, sometimes even centuries. It is difficult to see how a movement driving secession of an entire province from South Africa could avoid the same fate.

There are also many unanswered questions. Even if secession in South Africa were legally and politically possible, and especially if the political economy of an independent Cape were to flourish, as secessionists believe it will, it is hard to imagine how this new state would defend its very long borders, under the pressure of southward migration, as desperate people seek to escape failing states to the north in search of better opportunities.

Even the Mediterranean Sea has proved a weak barrier between North Africa and Europe, as economic and political refugees seek a better life.

Although self-determination in an independent country is a highly emotive and appealing prospect for minorities in South Africa, an objective analysis shows that it is simply not achievable, for the foreseeable future, in the real world.

This leaves us with the final response to a failing state:

Building a New Political Majority in South Africa

This is a hard and difficult road, to which I have devoted most of my adult life, because it is the only viable long-term solution compatible with our Constitution and the challenges of building a nation out of disparate and divided elements, after centuries of conflict.

While the need to find common ground across barriers is an immediate and pressing necessity in Southern Africa, it is also rapidly becoming a major challenge for the rest of the world.

Despite the resurgence of racial and ethnic nationalism, symbolised by international developments as divergent as America's Culture Wars and Britain's Brexit, the world is a shrinking place.

Almost every country and continent is going to have to find ways in which people of different cultures and backgrounds can live together in the same polity while respecting a foundational set of rules and conventions that ensure sustained progress and opportunities for everyone.

The history of successful democracies shows what the essentials are: A respect for constitutionalism and freedom within the rule of law; a capable State underpinned by a commitment to meritocracy; a societal culture of accountability; and a market-based economy, with social safety nets for the vulnerable.

It is these values and institutions that have enabled Western democracies to succeed and improve the opportunities and life chances of their citizens, while ensuring the resilience necessary to weather storms and resolve conflicts without resorting to authoritarian rule.

This approach is also entirely compatible with other responses to South Africa's crisis, already highlighted in this chapter in various forms of self-reliance. Indeed, strong civil society organisations, such as the Solidarity Movement among Afrikaners, and the independent initiatives of the private sector, are necessary conditions for democracy's success.

Building a new political majority in South Africa is an alternative to secession. It strongly supports greater autonomy for provinces, cities, and towns, so that those who have voted for an alternative to ANC rule can feel the positive impact of their decisions. This is a battle well-worth engaging and entirely winnable.

The more the ANC's racial nationalism fails, the more important and possible it becomes to demonstrate that alternative policies can work. This requires the greatest possible autonomy for cities and towns, and the one province the ANC does not govern.

It also requires a highly competent alternative. Lessons from other African countries teach us that the "liberation parties" usually wither away, but that their electoral replacements often turn out to be as bad – or even worse. That is why the greatest threat to a country's long term prospects occurs when the opposition becomes as bad and as venal as the government.

Ultimately voters must inevitably learn the hard way, through experiencing the consequences of their decisions.

Of course, the foundation stones that underpin functional democracies are not value-free or culturally agnostic. They are rooted in the history of Western Enlightenment, and we have to be bold enough to say so. In complex plural societies, they are often in conflict with traditional systems, where people are accountable to, and dependent on, the favour and patronage of their leaders, rather than the other way around.

This fundamental incompatibility is one of the aspects currently bedevilling South Africa's prospects. It is also one of the factors driving the woke form of "identity politics" and its sinister objective of convincing people that independent, democratic institutions of state are alien to their culture.

The DA, as South Africa's official opposition, has the job of defending these institutions and offering an alternative to the racial nationalism which has led to an unaccountable polity, endemic corruption, and the impoverishment of millions

We were working on this project long before the ANC came to power, indeed ever since a small group of liberal democrats broke away from the old and divided United Party in 1959 to form the Progressive Party in order to challenge the racist policies of the "whites-only" National Party.

For 13 years, the Progressive Party had only one Member of Parliament, Helen Suzman, who was the most vocal opponent of apartheid in the South African Parliament.

Slowly, through mergers with other smaller parties and a series of name changes, its successor, the Progressive Federal Party, became the official opposition in 1977. As all parties do, it suffered occasional setbacks, such as losing its official opposition status to the far-right Conservative Party in 1987.

Ironically, after playing a key role to ensure that fundamental liberal principles were included in the South African Constitution during the constitutional negotiations of the early 1990s, the party was crushed in South Africa's first democratic election, winning only 1,7% of the vote, and 6 Members of Parliament.

Under the leadership of Tony Leon, their performance so outstripped other opposition parties, that it regained the title of official opposition in the election of 1999, and despite setbacks, grew to become a party of government, first at local level, and eventually winning the province of the Western Cape in 2009, during my term as leader.

By 2014, it had garnered 59% of Western Cape votes, and in 2016 a two thirds majority in the City of Cape Town. It also managed to convincingly break out of the Western Cape, establishing coalition governments in three other major cities — Port Elizabeth, Johannesburg, and the capital, Pretoria.

There is an unwritten rule in politics: you are at your most vulnerable when you have just achieved your greatest success.

It was at this critical juncture, around 2015/16 that the woke virus began to reach epidemic proportions in South Africa. From its epicentre in the United States, it infected our universities, and spread rapidly through the pervasive reach of social media.

The DA's new young leadership had no immunity or defence mechanisms against the noxious idea that racial categorisation, in the search for equality of outcomes, was a progressive notion. They fell for it. And alienated a considerable component of the party's support base in the process.

That necessitated an internal shake-up, including a change of leadership, which duly followed the electoral setback of 2019.

The DA is now well on the way to strengthening its foundations so that we can resume our growth path on the basis of the only formula that can work in the long term: respect for the rights of autonomous individuals to live in freedom, form communities of their choice, and advance their lives without violating the rights of others under a Constitution which ensures that independent state institutions defend these rights.

Yet, we accept that while this classical liberal formulation is necessary, it is insufficient to compensate for centuries of past injustice.

The big question is how to ensure restitution for past wrongs without resurrecting the policies that gave rise to injustice and conflict in the first place — racial classification, racial domination and preferencing, and the denial of individual liberty.

That is why our new Economic Justice Policy has been such a turning point, both for our party, and in the longer term, for South Africa. It represents the first time any political party has put forward a comprehensive policy to address the legacy of centuries of economic exclusion while simultaneously freeing South Africa from apartheid race classification.

This is a big deal. The woke media were horrified at our non-racial approach to economic restitution, but over time, no doubt, reality will dawn that one cannot overcome the legacy of racist policies by replacing them with more racist policies.

Our Economic Justice Policy also recognises that colonialism and apartheid are not the only reasons for the crisis of poverty and unemployment that South Africa faces. The 27 years of ANC rule have played their own devastating role.

The policy, authored by the head of our Policy Unit, Gwen Ngwenya, therefore focuses on the root causes of inequality of opportunity and socio-economic deprivation, using the United Nations Sustainable Development Goals as the framework for redress.

It requires the whole of society to address any combination of the 17 goals most suited to their context and mandate, within a framework that will measure overall social and economic progress.

And crucially, it uses poverty and other indicators to measure deprivation and disadvantage — not race. Although there is still a massive overlap between race and poverty in South Africa, deprivation can be measured (in and of itself) and does not need race as a proxy.

Already there is an entire welfare system — including pensions and child grants — that is based on need, not race, making it entirely possible to extend this principle to other forms of redress.

The only blockage is a voracious political elite who see their chances of self-enrichment slipping away if race is removed as a proxy for disadvantage.

If the "race proxy" goes, they will have nothing to justify their continued access to the state's largesse in the issuing of tenders and contracts. Their cover for corruption would vanish.

However, appeals to racial and ethnic solidarity continue to convince voters that racial preferencing is in their interests too — when all the available evidence demonstrates the opposite.

Using the globally-recognised model of the United Nations Sustainable Development Goals to provide a scorecard of progress for South Africa could provide a model for other countries too, ones that are grappling with deep fissures of inequality.

Our core challenge is to convince the voters that this approach is preferable. But offering policy solutions to complex problems is far less compelling than emotive appeals to ethnic and racial solidarity, and scapegoating minorities — especially in a complex plural society with one foot in a highly developed industrial economy, and the other in traditional forms of feudal land tenure, governed by traditional chieftaincies.

Before the ANC is beaten at the ballot box, it will continue its slow-motion implosion as its competing criminal syndicates battle for control of the state's patronage machine.

The ANC is unsalvageable.

There comes a point in the life of an organisation when it is so riven with corruption that it is impossible to take decisive steps to fix it because almost everyone with any power, at every level, is implicated.

As Bathabile Dlamini famously said in an inimitable South African way: "We all have our *smallanyana* skeletons".

The world *smallanyana* is a delightful portmanteau word, fusing "small" with the Nguni suffix *"nyana"* — also meaning small. It doesn't mean the skeletons are doubly small. It means there are many of them.

The ANC's disintegration will herald a period of profound instability — and no one can predict with any certainty how things will turn out. But slowly, the choices and consequences will become crystal clear — an authoritarian racial-nationalism, centralising all power in the hands of a political elite, versus an open, non-racial, increasingly federal alternative, based on constitutionalism, individual freedom, and a social market economy.

That is the real choice facing South Africans.

As the ANC's gigantic edifice collapses, the dust and noise it emits will initially obscure these stark choices. And there is also no guarantee that constitutionalism will prevail.

The only hope that it will lies in the strength of the democratic alternative — underpinned by a vibrant, resilient and independent civil society, as well as significant areas of the country under local or provincial DA governance (currently about 8 million people) with substantially greater autonomy.

A strong contender on the other extreme will be the populist, ultra-nationalists, exemplified by Julius Malema's Economic Freedom Fighters, who will make common cause with kindred spirits inside the ANC as the party unravels.

And, as the ANC approaches its next elective Congress scheduled for 2022, there is a likelihood that Cyril Ramaphosa will turn out to be a one-term president. Succession battles in the ANC often trigger splintering, and this one will be no exception.

The question is: will it be the catalytic moment that results in a fundamental realignment of South African politics?

No one can say for sure, but what is entirely predictable is that South Africa's existential crisis will continue in the decade ahead. We are used to it. As far back as anyone can remember, our clock has been stuck at five minutes to midnight.

Jan Smuts, renowned South African statesman, military leader, philosopher, and twice Prime Minister of the former Union of South Africa, once famously said "South Africa is a country in which the best and the worst never happen".

I am not sure whether he made this observation before or after the crucial 1948 election when his United Party lost power to the National Party, that then began to conceptualise and later impose, apartheid.

But it is true that South Africa is a country with a remarkable depth of resilience that has been able to meet almost every challenge thrown at it.

Since my days in journalism, as an anti-apartheid activist, and a politician seeking to grow the liberal, democratic alternative to racial nationalism, I have worked with people from all backgrounds and walks of life. Much of my time and energy has been spent in South Africa's poorest communities where I developed life-long bonds and friendships, and experienced first-hand the realistic pragmatism, decency and humanity of ordinary South Africans.

This makes it all the more puzzling that these positive attributes are often so quickly eroded when people assume positions of authority. Power is all too often regarded as a licence to extract obeisance and resources from others and advantages for oneself.

Indeed, there is a poor alignment between traditional systems of "big man" rule and the core tenets of constitutional democracies. Despite this, I have faith that the innate sense of fairness and justice manifested by so many in our country, will constitute the "critical mass" required to enable constitutionalism to triumph in the end.

South Africa matters. Its success is not only important to its people, but to the African continent. And the world.

We are at the cutting edge of what a complex, plural society looks like. If we fail to find a way of living together in a free society (rather than a fear society), the challenge will not evaporate. It will continue to haunt a growing number of countries across the globe. That is why our prospects arouse such interest and hold such significance.

Our success matters. It requires facing facts, having the difficult conversations, understanding what freedom means, why it is important, and how to nurture and defend it. It also means being ready to fight for it, when necessary.

Wokeness is making it increasingly difficult to do these basic, essential things. Which is why I wrote this book. If Wokeness wins, whatever it is called by then, at least I want to know that I made every effort to raise the alarm.

If the moderate non-racial liberal constitutionalists manage to emerge triumphant, we could be an enormous resource for the Western world facing the same challenges.

As always, I believe that in South Africa, The Worst will not happen, because enough of us continue to work for The Best.

About the Author

Helen Zille, best-selling author, path-breaking journalist, and anti-apartheid activist, has had a profound impact on South African politics during the past two decades in various roles. These include her election as Leader of the Opposition Democratic Alliance (DA) (2007-2015), Executive Mayor of the City of Cape Town (when she was awarded the World Mayor accolade), and Premier of the Western Cape Province (where she served with distinction for two consecutive terms). In November 2020 she was elected Chairperson of the DA's Federal Council.

She defines her guiding political philosophy as "classical liberalism" and has during her years in politics, pursued the ends of liberal social justice. She believes that "critical social justice" (otherwise known as Wokeness) will result in a failed state and a steady escalation of mass impoverishment in South Africa.

This book explains why.

Notes

1. Splashed by the Woke Spittoon

1. The account of this encounter has been taken from multiple media sources. The author made several attempts to contact Ashleigh personally via her social media profiles and by visiting a restaurant cited as her most recent place of work. Ashleigh has not been active on social media for a while, and attempts to reach her via these attempts did not succeed. As the media accounts had been consistent across media platforms, and have not been denied, they were accepted as valid for the purpose of this account.
2. The use of the multiple pronouns is necessary when referring to a "trans" person, if one does not know what their choice of pronoun is, according to Woke convention.
3. Quoted from "Anti-Racist Structuralists and Non-Racist Culturalists" Quillette, 13 September 2020.

2. Delving Deeper into Wokeness

1. https://en.wikipedia.org/wiki/Mfecane#:~:text=How%20many%20people%20died%20as,%2C%22%20concluded%20Professor%20John%20Wright.

3. The Great Betrayal

1. At the time of writing, Letlape was the Deputy Vice-Chancellor responsible for Strategic Services at the University of Johannesburg.
2. There are many examples that illustrate this insidious phenomenon. Two recent books that give an insight into how this works are *Gangster State: Unravelling Ace Magashule's Web of Capture* (Penguin Random House) by Pieter-Louis Myburgh and *VBS: A Dream Defrauded* (Penguin Random House) by Dewald van Rensburg.

4. Caging Minds

1. www.educonnect.co.za
2. *Cynical Theories. How Universities Made Everything about Race, Gender and Identity – And Why This Harms Everybody* (Swift Press, 2020) Helen Pluckrose and James Lindsay.

7. Why SA Won't Survive Wokeness

1. www.tradingeconomics.com
2. See:
   https://rationalstandard.com/affirmative-action-sa-ended-immediately/
   https://www.news24.com/news24/MyNews24/Why-Affirmative-Action-is-necessary-20120317
   https://themediaonline.co.za/2019/01/while-the-anc-is-in-power-sa-has-no-chance-of-recovering/
3. "Four Fallacies of the Woke Prohibition of Cultural Arguments", David Bern, Nov 21 2020, in *New Discourses*.

Printed in Great Britain
by Amazon